AF540712

MANAGEMENT
OF
WORKING CAPITAL

MANAGEMENT
OF
WORKING CAPITAL

By

Dr. S.D. Talekar
Reader in Commerce
L.B.S. College, Partur
District Jalna (Maharashtra)
(India)

DISCOVERY PUBLISHING HOUSE
NEW DELHI-110002

First Published-2005
Reprinted: 2013
ISBN 81-7141-962-3

Published by

DISCOVERY PUBLISHING HOUSE
4831/24, Ansari Road, Prahlad Street,
Darya Ganj, New Delhi-110002 (India)
Phone: 23279245 • Fax: 91-11-23253475
E-mail:dphtemp@indiatimes.com

Printed at:
Dynamic printers, Delhi

Preface

The efficient and effective management of working capital enables a firm to maximise profitability and also to maintain adequate liquidity in the business. The manner of the management of working capital determines to a large extent the success or failure of an enterprise. Many a time, in the event of failure of business enterprise, inadequate working capital is given out its main reason. But in the ultimate evaluation it may be the mismanagement of working capital. Working capital is as important in a business as blood in the human body. Insufficient working capital creates trouble in smooth functioning of day to day business operations which also affect profitability.

Sugar industry being an important agro-based industry, next to textile, plays predominant role in the national economy. The industry accounts for a massive investment of over Rs. 2500 crores and provides employment to about 5 lakh workers. About 5.5 million farmers are engaged in cane cultivation. Agro-based industry like co-operative sugar factory have large potentials of creating employment in the rural area. The experience in co-operative sugar factory in Maharashtra has proved that, the agriculture processing units in co-operative sector if managed well, can provide good scope for rural development.

In spite of this success the co-operative sugar industry in Maharashtra is facing various problems and has become a centre of criticism due to several reasons. The co-operative sugar factories in the state are lagging behind in management efficiency. They are not able to control their cost, hence major co-operative sugar factories in the state and particularly in Marathwada region are carrying huge losses. Considering the significance of working capital management in maintaining profitability and financial strength and equally considering the significant role of co-operative sugar in the economic life of Marathwada region, the problem entitled 'management of working capital in sugar co-operatives' is undertaken for detail study. In the present study attempt has been made to study the management of working capital in sugar co-operatives in the Marathwada and tries to find out the short term financial strength and weaknesses of co-operative sugar factories in the region.

The study is being presented in eight chapters:

1. The first chapter deals with the general background of sugar industries in India, Maharastra and Marathwada;
2. The second chapter is devoted to review the relevant and recent literature on the sugar industry;
3. The third chapter deals with the brief history of each co-operative sugar factory selected under study;
4. Chapter IV presents trends and liquidity analysis of working capital in sugar co-operatives;
5. Fifth chapter discuss the inventory management;
6. Sixth chapter deals with receivable management;
7. In chapter VII cash position of the selected sugar factories have been analysed;
8. The last chapter summarises the conclusions of the present study and offers suggestions for the improvement of efficiency and effectiveness of working capital management.

The present study covers the total period of ten years, i.e. from 1991-92 to 2000- 01.

Fourteen co-operative sugar factories are selected as sample unit from the Marathwada region.

Acknowledgements

I am deeply indebted to my guide Dr. G.A. Nikam, Director, Professor Dept. of Management Science, Dr.Babasaheb Ambedkar Marathwada University, Aurangabad, without whose learned guidance and inspiration, this work would not have been completed.

I wish to acknowledge my indebtedness to the librarian and library staff of Dr. Babasaheb Ambedkar Marathwada University Library, Aurangabad for their co-operation. I also express my sense of gratitude to officials of Regional Joint Director (Sugar) Aurangabad and Nanded for providing me the required statistical data.

I am very much thankful to Managing Directors, Chief Accountants and their staff of all the co-operative sugar factories covered in the study, for providing me annual reports, statistical data and necessary information.

I am also thankful to Dr. D.P. Takale, Prof. A.B. Waykar, Prof. S.N. Chavan, Prof. S.S. Muley, Dr. B.T. Dirange, Prof. D.R. Manwar for their constant encouragement.

The researcher is thankful to Shri. Babasaheb Akat, President M.S.S.P. Mandal, Partur, Dr. B.B. Dhaneshwar, Principal, L.B.S. College, Partur for encouraging to complete the present book. I equally thankful to all my colleagues for their inspiration from time to time.

I am indebted to my beloved father Dagduji Talekar, mother Kasabai Talekar, brothers Nayabrao and Babasaheb, father-in-law Baburao Jadhav, brother-in-law Sarjerao Jadhav and Vishnu Jadhav who have been a constant source of inspiration and encouragement in the successful completion of this book.

I am thankful to my wife Mrs. Chandrakala, nephew Karbhari, daughter Seema, Sushma and son Rahul who had to sacrifice a large number of affectionate moments because of this research work.

I am thankful to Shri Santosh Pawar of Dynamic Computers who carefully typed this research work.

Dr. S. D. Talekar
L.B.S. College, Partur

Contents

Contents

1

Introduction

Sugar industry in recent times has acquired great significance in India. It has been developing by leaps and bounds. The sugar industry is second largest agro-based industry in India. From this point of view its contribution to the national wealth and employment generation cannot be set aside. The effective administration of working capital helps in understanding the survival and growth of sugar industry. Apart from this, many a times, problem arises as to how effectively the working capital be managed to obtain the results in terms of higher return on investment. Very often paucity of working capital is considered as the potent factor for the failure of a unit.

The Co-operative Sugar industry has been playing a pivotal role in the development of rural Maharashtra. The real boost to Co-operative Sugar industry came with setting up of the first Co-operative Sugar factory at Loni in Ahmednagar district in 1950 under the imaginative leadership of late Prof. D.R. Gadgil and Vikhe Patil. This was the first experiment of its own kind in India. The success inspired the farmers in the state and nation and it also inspired the State and Central Government. People and Government recognised the significance of a Co-operative Sugar factory in the rural economic development and growth of Co-operative Sugar factories started in Maharashtra. The realistic support of state and Central government has contributed equally in the progress of Co-operative Sugar industry. The State of Maharashtra has maintained its leading position in Co-operative Sugar industry since its beginning. Co-operative Sugar industry in Maharashtra has got a place of pride in the Sugar industry in India and contributes a big share in the growth of Co-operative Sugar factories and in the production of Sugar.

Development of Sugar Industry in India

British Government of India introduced the co-operative ideology in 1885 for solving the credit needs of the farmers in this country as per the recommendations of Mr. Nicholson, the officer from Punjab province who was asked to visit the West Germany for studying the problems. Even the British Indian Government realised that the co-operation was the way to solve the problems of the peasants in this country. The first act to promote the co-operative societies and to regulate them was passed in 1904 known as "Co-operative Credit Societies Act 1904", which was amended in 1912. The subject of co-operation was transferred from central list to the concurrent list in 1919 and thereafter the provincial states passed their enactment to promote and regulate Co-operative movement in the state. The Bombay province co-operative societies Act was passed in 1925, which laid down "Co-operation as a way of life for better living, better business and better methods of production". Because of all these efforts, the co-operatives entered in many economic activities, though with slow pace during pre-independence period.

After independence, the Government of India laid down the definite approach towards the co-operative movement in furtherance of their objective to remove inequalities and the establishment of socialistic pattern of society. The Government of India appointed a committee under the chairmanship of Shri Gorwala in 1951, which is well known as All India Rural Credit Survey Committee. This committee submitted its report in 1954, making far reaching recommendations to revamp the co-operative credit structure in this country. This committee made recommendations to promote the co-operative processing societies of farmers and linking of agricultural credit with agricultural marketing.

The committee made the observation and expressed its views that "co-operation has failed but co-operation must succeed". The Government of India has accepted most of the recommendations of the committee and took steps to implement the same. The commitment of Government of India to promote co-operative movement and to accept it as a way to bring socialistic pattern of society in this country is reflected in the entire plan document right from the first five-year plan.

The Government of India's policy towards co-operative movement was very much responsible for the development of sugar industry in Co-operative sector after independence. According to Ajit Prasad Jain, former minister for food and agriculture, Government of India, "the dawn of independence in 1947 brought its wake a change in the outlook and policy of the nation. Our vowed objective is removal of inequalities and early establishment of a socialistic pattern of society. One of the ways for achieving this objective is to encourage peasants to organise and manage processing industries based on the crops produced by them. The establishment of the large number of growers Co-operative Sugar factories is an effort in that direction."[1] The Government of India appointed working groups, committees, etc. to make suggestions for development of the Co-operative Sugar industries through their various policies including licensing, fixing cane and sugar price and other controls over the Sugar industry.

With all their hard and sincere efforts, they succeeded in establishing a sound co-operative movement in the Sugar industry. "The first Co-operative Sugar factory, which was established at Etikoppka in Andhra Pradesh though survived, it does not seem to have inspired the development of Co-operative Sugar factories in India. The credit for initiating this scheme of development of co-operative Sugar factories should go to the Pravaranagar co-operative sugar factory established in 1948."[2]

Development of Sugar Industries in Maharashtra

First Sugar factory in Maharashtra was established in 1919 in private sector which was started by British Company at Haregaon in Ahemadnagar district[3]. No effort was made to organise the co-operative sugar factories in the old Bombay State, which is a part of the Maharashtra state now, till 1947. It was only in 1948, the first co-operative sugar factory was established in Ahamednagar district at Pravaranagar. The establishment of co-operative sugar factory at Pravaranagar in 1948 was itself very good beginning and thereafter many co-operative sugar factories were developed in the State of Maharashtra.

In the words of Maharashtra Economic Development Council, "The vast smiling green fields of sugarcane which are seen in Maharashtra today were the success of this co-operative sugar factories, created tremendous upsurge amongst the sugarcane growers of the state to organise more and more co-operative sugar factories. The co-operative sugar factories in the state have brought about a change in the cropping pattern and through the introduction of better varieties of cane have succeeded in improving substantially the cane yield in their areas and can proudly claim to have obtained the highest recovery among all sugar factories co-operative or joint stock. Along with the technological achievements, they have also infused on the atmosphere other powerful social and economic forces, so that the co-operative sugar factories in the state have today came to be regarded as effective spring boards for achieving rural development."[4]

The rapid growth of sugar industry in Maharashtra has helped to a very great extent in stabilising the sugar production in the country and reducing the chronic shortage of sugar. Maharashtra produces about 36% of the total sugar produced in the country and rank second to Uttar Pradesh[5]. In 2000-01 there were 134 co-operative sugar factories in the co-operative sector and all have been set up at a fairly high block cost compared to the private sugar factories. It is now an accomplished fact that the soil and climate condition of Maharashtra state are favourable for the plantation of sugarcane. The state is located in tropical belt. This belt is famous all over the world as it consists of most suitable areas for raising sugarcane crop. Majority of the countries producing sugar are situated in this belt. On account of this geographically advantageous position, Maharashtra is known as 'sugar bowl' of the country[6].

In Maharashtra the real boost to the sugar industry came with the setting of the first co-operative sugar factory at Loni in Ahamednagar district in 1950, under the inspiring and imaginative leadership of late D.R. Gadgil and Shri Vikhe Patil. The success of this co-operative Sugar factory created tremendous enthusiasm amongst the sugarcane growers in the state to organise more and more co-operative sugar factories. Table 1.1 gives an idea about development of co-operative sugar factories in Maharashtra.

In 1950-51 there was only one co-operative sugar factory in the state at Pravaranagar and total 14 sugar factories including 13 in private sector. In the same year in India there were only two co-operative sugar factories. In 1960-61 the co-operative sugar factories in India were 30 and in Maharashtra they were 14. There was a substantial increase in co-operative sugar factories in Maharashtra after the industrial policy resolution 1956. In 1960-61 the production of sugar in co-operative factories in India was 450 thousand tons while in Maharashtra it was 264 thousand tons, which was 56% of India's total. In the decade of 1960-1970 the number of co-operative sugar factories in the state gone to 30 and sugar production increased to 773 thousand tons which was 61% of the total sugar production in co-operative sector in India. In the year 1980-81 the total sugar factories in the state were 77 out of which 67 were in co-operative sector. In the same year total sugar production of the state was 2085 thousand tons out of which 1877 thousand tons was of co-operative sector. In the year 1990-91 there were 220 co-operative sugar factories in India and 93 were in Maharashtra. In the same year only 4 factories remained in private sector in Maharashtra as in a span of ten years near about nine factories in private sector converted into co-operative sector. In the year 1997-98 Maharashtra occupied 62% share in total production of sugar in co-operative sector in India. In this year there were 220 sugar factories in co-operative sector in India out of which 93 factories were in Maharashtra. Total sugar production of co-operative sector in India was 6050 thousand tons and the share of Maharashtra's co-operative sector was 3746 thousand tons which comes to 62% . In the year 2000-01 there were 259 co-operative sugar factories in India out of which 128 were in Maharashtra which produced 6705 thousand tons of sugar which is 62% of total sugar production by all co-operative sugar factories in India.

Table—1.1: Co-operative Sugar Factories in India and Maharashtra

Year	*Co-op. Sugar Factories in India*	*Co.op. Sugar Factories in Maharashtra*	*% Share Maharashtra*	*Sugar Production of Co.op. Sugar Factories in India*	*Sugar Production of Co.op. Sugar Factories in Maharashtra*	*% Share of Maharashtra on Total*
1950-51	02 (140)	01 (14)	50			
1960-61	30 (143)	14 (27)	47	450 (3028)	264 (1000)	58
1970-71	73 (215)	30 (41)	41	1262 (4350)	773 (1155)	61
1980-81	149(315)	67 (77)	44	2993 (5150)	1877 (2085)	63
1990-91	220(385)	93 (97)	42	7274 (12047)	4010 (4119)	55
1991-92	224(392)	94 (99)	42	7838 (13405)	4091 (4218)	52
1992-93	224(393)	95 (99)	42	6424 (10609)	3306 (3360)	51
1993-94	222(394)	94 (99)	42	5655 (9833)	2699 (2746)	48
1994-95	231(408)	104 (107)	45	8655 (14643)	4923 (5025)	57
1995-96	232(416)	106 (109)	46	9642 (16453)	5263 (5394)	55
1996-97	229(412)	102 (105)	45	6982 (12905)	3360 (3445)	48
1997-98	222(400)	92 (95)	41	7062 (12852)	3746 (3847)	57
1998-99	249(427)	117 (120)	47	8972 (15539)	5216 (5338)	58
1999-00	251(423)	119 (123)	47	10369 (18200)	6350 (6503)	61
2000-01	259(436)	128 (137)	49	10499 (18511)	6477 (6705)	62

Source: *(i)* Bhartiya sugar directory & year book 1987.

(ii) Co-operative sugar, March 2002, Vol. 33. p. 594, 598.

Note: Figures in the brackets indicate total No. of Sugar Factories and production of Private & Co-operative Sector.

Development of Sugar Industry in Marathwada

The Marathwada region was a part of Hyderabad state under Nizam till its merger with the old Bombay state in 1948. The first sugar factory was established in 1957 by M/s Dhoot in private sector in Marathwada at Gangapur of Aurangabad district. It was passed on from M/s Dhoot to M/s W.H. Brady & Co., who in turn sold the unit to M/s Belapur Sugar Mills Ltd. This factory was converted to Co-operative sector in 1968. This was the beginning of the co-operative movement in sugar industry in Marathwada area.

By the end of 1985, there were 22 co-operative sugar factories in Marathwada of which 18 were in production and 4 were in the stage of erection. Of these 4 units which were in erection stage during 1985, all were likely to go into production within a year time, i.e. by the middle of 1986-87. At present there are 36 sugar factories in Marathwada region. Marathwada, a backward region of Maharashtra state has good potentials for sugarcane cultivation and development of sugar industry because the land of Marathwada is very fertile and the climate is suitable for growing sugarcane crop. Sugar industry adds to the income of the farmers, provides casual and permanent employment, helps to earn foreign exchange and also helps to develop various kinds of ancillary and by-product industries. This leads to good industrial and economic development of the region.

Development of Co-operative Sugar Factories in Marathwada

Sl. No.	*Name of District*	*No. of Factories*
1.	Aurangabad	7
2.	Jalna	3
3.	Beed	6
4.	Parbhani	5
5.	Nanded	6
6.	Osmanabad	3
7.	Latur	6
	Total	**36**

Source: Performance of sugar factories in Maharashtra 2001-02.

Government and Co-operative Sugar Industry

Sugar industry is the largest industry in which co-operative form is largely used. Considering the significance of sugar in the life of human beings, sugar industry is rigidly controlled by the Government of India and the rules and regulations are equally applicable to the factories in co-operative, private and public sector. The review of central and state governments policies should be taken separately.

Central Government's Policy

Central Government regulates almost all aspects of sugar industry such as fixing of cane price, quality, storage and release of sugar stocks, fixing of sugar price and by-products, payment of wages and salaries, proportion of levy sugar and free sale sugar and financing of sugar co-operatives. The major elements of government policy which govern the functioning of sugar industry may be listed as follows :

(a) Licensing policy

(b) Financing policy

(c) Pricing policy

(d) Distribution policy

(a) Licensing Policy

Since independence the Government of India has been implementing licensing policy for installation of new units and for expansion of existing units by applying ad hoc licensing committees as per the Provisions of Industries (Development and Regulation) Act 1951. These committees were issuing licenses according to the provisions of said act and under the guidelines given by planning commission in the five year plans.

The licenses were issued by considering targets of sugar production as set by planning commission, after considering domestic consumption, exports and buffer stocks.

India adopted new economic policy in 1991. The broad features of this policy were liberalisation, globalisation and privatisation. The first stage of economic reforms was started in 1991 but licensing policy for sugar industry remained unchanged.

In second stage of implementation of economic reforms the Government delicensed the sugar industry. The Government's decision of delicensing was declared on 20th August 1998. As per this decision the licensing norms were relaxed for establishment of new mills. However, new mills were subjected to condition that these would have to be located at least 15 kms from any existing one for ensuring assured supply of sugarcane. The license is issued on submission of Industrial Entrepreneur Memorandum (IEM). The existing sugar mills have also been exempted from licensing for their expansion. The location condition of 25 kms is brought down to 15 kms. Though licensing norms were relaxed, entrepreneurs wishing to start new units were required to fulfil certain obligations including getting certificate from state government on cane availability and tying up with financial institutions for capital.

(b) Financing Policy

Financing policy for fixed capital and working capital may be separately discussed as follows:

(i) Fixed Capital Finance

In order to encourage co-operative sector in sugar industry, a scheme of financing co-operative sugar factories was introduced. Under this, the state government participate in the share capital of co-operative sugar factories and the central and state governments are to guarantee the loan advanced to the factories by financial institutions like IFCI, IDBI, ICICI, etc. To enable the state governments to participate in the share capital of co-operative sugar factories, NCDC advances loan to them out of the funds placed at its disposal by the central government. The brief review of the pattern of financing project cost since 1960 is shown in Table 1.2.

In 1960 the project cost of 1250 TCD capacity unit was Rs. 90 lakhs and debt to equity ratio was 65:35[7]. Out of 35% equity, the state governments contribution was 25% and members contribution was 10%. In 1970, the project cost of the same capacity unit increased to Rs. 270 lakhs but the debt equity ratio and proportion of states contribution to members contribution in share capital remained same. In 1980, the project cost increased to

Rs. 750 lakhs and debt equity ratio also changed to 60:40. The state governments contribution in equity capital was almost same, 30% to 40%, and members contribution was 10% to 15%[8]. In 1985 the project cost of 1250 TCD capacity unit was Rs. 1050 lakhs but the debt equity ratio and internal proportion of state governments capital and members capital was same. In 1989 project cost of 2500 TCD unit was Rs. 3500 to 3800 lakhs[9]. The normative cost fixed by central government was Rs. 3400 lakhs. The debt equity ratio was same i.e. 60:40, but state government revised the internal proportion of contribution in equity capital and higher contribution of state was given to the co-operative sugar factories coming up in industrially backward districts[10]. Since 1985 a co-operative sugar factory of 2500 TCD was taken as economically viable and recommended by state government for granting license. In 1995 the project cost of 2500 TCD capacity unit tremendously increased to Rs. 4000 to 4200 lakhs, but normative cost was fixed by central government was Rs. 4000 lakhs. The debt equity ratio was same with proportion of members capital to state government's capital. In 1998 the project cost increased to Rs 4700 to 4800 lakhs and the normative cost was fixed as Rs. 4500 lakhs, other proportions were same.

(ii) Working Capital Finance

The working capital finance is provided by state level co-operative bank and district central co-operative banks, under the guarantee of state government. It is generally provided for a period of one year as per the working capital requirement given by the co-operative sugar factory. Two types of working capital finance are provided to co-operative sugar factories.

The clean cash credit is allowed to every sugar factory for making pre-seasonal arrangement. This finance of working capital is called as pre-seasonal finance. This finance is required for payment of advance to harvesting and transport, labour, purchasing of gunny bags and chemicals etc. Second type of working capital finance is 'seasonal finance'. During crushing season the payment to sugarcane growers, salary and wages and expenditure on harvesting and transport of sugarcane requires huge amount.

Table—1.2: Financing Pattern for Project Cost of Co-operative Sugar Factories

Period	*Project Capacity TCD*	*Project Cost Rs. Lakhs*	*Normative Cost Fixed by Central Govt. Rs. Lakhs*	*Debt to Equity Ratio for Financing Project Cost (Percentage)*			*Total*
				Debt	*Equity*		
					Members	*State*	
1950	1250	90.00	–	65%	–	–	–
1970	1250	270.00	–	65%	10%	25%	100%
1980	1250	750.00	–	60%	10% to 15%	25%	100%
1985	1250	1050.00	–	60%	10% to 15%	30% to 40%	100%
1989	2500	3500 to 3800	3400	60%	10% to 15%	30% to 40%	100%
1995	2500	4000 to 4200	4000	60%	10% to 15%	30% to 40%	100%
1998	2500	4700 to 4800	4500	60%	10% to 15%	30% to 40%	100%

Source: 1. Miss Sangeeta R. Kurulkar, Ph.D. unpublished thesis, p. 122.

2. G. Guar—Co-operative sugar, Jan. 1999, p. 410.

3. R.M. Kharche—Sugar Co-operative in Developing Economy, p. 85.

(c) Pricing Policy

Pricing policy of co-operative sugar factories can be divided into two parts.

(i) Pricing of sugarcane

(ii) Pricing of sugar

(i) Pricing of Sugarcane

Sugarcane pricing policy is important as it affects the area under sugarcane and production of sugarcane. In co-operative sector the machanism for determining sugarcane price to be actually paid, does not depend on market forces of supply and demand. It is determined on the basis of democratic principle of equity and equality. In co-operative sugar factories sugarcane price is nothing but distribution of surplus, over and above all expenses of sugar production, to sugarcane suppliers in proportion to sugarcane supplied by them.[11] Since 1934 the government interferes in fixation of sugarcane price by way of fixation of minimum price to protect the interests of sugarcane growers. The co-operative sugar factories are not allowed to pay cane price less than the minimum price fixed by central government. This price of sugarcane is called as Statutory Minimum Price (SMP). While fixing SMP, the central government considers the cost of production, recovery of sugar from sugarcane, the availability of sugar and the return to the grower from alternative crops and trend of prices of agriculture commodities. From 1962-63 Central Government linked statutory minimum price with basic sugar recovery percentage with a premium on every 0.1% rise in the recovery over basic recovery.[12] While fixing price the central government is guided by the recommendations of agricultural price commission, state governments and by the views of cane growers and sugar industry. The minimum cane price is being fixed with the object of ensuring payment of a guaranteed price for cane by sugar factories to cane growers.

(ii) Pricing of Sugar

In 1952-53 Directorate of Sugar was set up by central government and control of sugar price and distribution was taken over by central government. Whenever the sugar production in the country is decreased and the sugar stocks were low, the government imposed control on sugar release and price. On the other hand, when the sugar production was more than the expected level, the Government did not fix any ex-factory price of sugar. In 1958 Government adopted other measures for effective control of availability of sugar to all the people. As per these measures the wholesale dealers were licensed by state Government. A specific quota was assigned to individual states and inter-state movement of sugar was banned. This controls the price and distribution of sugar so as to enable the consumer to purchase sugar at reasonable price.

The fixing of ex-factory price sets a limitation on the price payable to cane growers. During the period of control, the cane prices do not exceed SMPs which were not much remunerative. Hence there was a decline in the area under sugarcane cultivation and consequently sugarcane output. This in turn affected sugar production. It was feared that due to controls imposed by the Government on sugar industry, the production of sugar may fall and may even fall short of internal demand. So it was realised that in order to induce farmers to cultivate cane, higher cane price than the minimum statutory price should be paid. This was not possible under ex-factory sugar price control. Therefore, in 1967 a system of partial decontrol of sugar was announced.

Under this partial decontrol policy, 60% of the production of sugar was procured by the government at a fixed levy price for public distribution system and 40% of the production of factory was free to sell in free market subject to release quota sanctioned by the government to the factories. The levy price is calculated on the basis of statutory minimum price and 'free price' is determined by market forces, which is always higher than levy price. The sale of 40% of the sugar output at higher price than levy price enabled the factories to pay higher cane prices to the farmers and attract more cane. The policy of partial decontrol attracted more cane growers and the output of sugarcane and sugar increased.

The levy price of sugar is fixed with the help of a committee of technical and costing experts. The committee refers to the data on the cost of production of sugar in different agro-climatic regions.[13] Table 1.3 gives an account of sugar pricing policy in different years.

(d) Distribution Policy

The Central Government also regulates the supply of sugar in the market. As discussed earlier, levy sale sugar quota is procured from co-operative sugar factories and distributed through public distribution system. Free sale sugar quota is sold in the market as per the government's release orders issued to factories on monthly basis. From January 1996 onwards, free sale quota of sugar factories is declared by Government on quarterly basis. The factories have to sell their free sale quota as per these directives. As per the Central Government Order date 27.8.98, the wholesale and retail stock of sugar are also regulated.[14] Stocks of sugar can be made to the limit of 1000 bags to 5000 bags as per the location of the cities.

Table—1.3: Sugar Pricing Policy in Different Years

Year	*Policy*	*Levy%*	*Free Sale%*
1967-68	Partial Control	60	40
1968-69	Partial Control	70	30
1969-70	Partial Control	70	30
1970-71	Partial Control	60	40*
(*a*) 1.10.70 to 24.5.71			
(*b*) 25.5.71 to 30.9.71	Decontrol		
1971-72	Decontrol		
(*a*) 1.10.71 to 31.12.71			
(*b*) 1.1.72 to 30.6.72	Scheme of Voluntary Distribution		
(*c*) 1.7.72 to 30.9.72	Partial Control	60	40*
1972-74	Partial Control	70*	30
1974-75 to 1977-78 (up to 15.8.78)	Partial Control	65	35
16.8.78 to 30.9.78	Decontrol		
1978-79	Scheme of		
(*a*) 1.10.78 to 11.9.79	Voluntary Distribution by Industry		
(*b*) 5.6.79 to 11.9.79	Monthly release Mechanism reintroduced by the Government		

(Contd...)

(c) 12.9.79 to 30.9.79	Full Price Control		
1979-80	Full Price Control		
(a) 1.10.79 to 16.12.79			
(b) 17.12.79 to 1984-85	Partial Control	65	35
1985-86	Partial Control	55	45
1986-87	Partial Control	50	50
1987-88	Partial Control	50	50
1988-89 to 1991-92	Partial Control	45	55
1992-93 to 1999-2000 (up to 31.12.99)	Partial Control	40	60
1999-2000 (from 1.1.2000)	Partial Control	30	70
2000-01 (up to 31.1.2001)	Partial Control	30	70
2000-01 (from 1.2.2001)	Partial Control	15	85

*: 3.5 % for export.

@: Decontrol for a part of the season.

Source: Co-operative sugar, July 2001. P. 959, Vol. 32, No. 11.

State Government's Policy

It may be stated that Government of Maharashtra has not spelt out any clear policy on establishment of new sugar factories or expansion of existing ones. However, the policy of state government in promoting new factories and expansion of exsiting factories is reflected in its various decisions. Brief review of state govts. policies may be as under:

(a) Licensing Policy

Licenses are issued to sugar factories by Central Government on the recommendation of State Government. As Maharashtra state is the pioneering state in co-operative sugar industry, it recommended various projects strongly to Central Government since 1948 like Pravaranagar project. The State Government recommends projects in the co-operative sector only. The growth of co-operative sugar factories in Maharashtra reflects the encouraging licensing policy of State Government. While recommending license to new units, the State Government has to ensure the supply of sugarcane. To ensure,the supply of sugarcane to new and existing units, State Government has set various regulations like zoning of area etc. The State Government is liberal in sanctioning co-operative sugar factories in backward areas.

(b) Financing Policy

The financing policy of the Government of Maharashtra is encouraging to co-operative sugar factories. Maharashtra is the first state in India to contribute a share capital in the co-operative sugar factory. From the very beginning the Government of Maharashtra has been providing a strong financial support to sugar co-operatives. In the project finances the state's contibution is about 30% to 35 % of the project cost as discussed earlier. The state government's share capital is granted against the redeemable preference shares. The amount is redeemable within 15 years[15]. The co-operative sugar factories have to create the share capital redemption fund and credit account every year, the amount equivalent of the instalment of government's share capital required to be redeemed. NCDC provides finance to State Governments to contibute in share capital.

(c) Pricing Policy

Though the statutory minimum price of sugarcane is fixed by Central Government, State Government also fixes minimum price higher than Central Government's price in the interest of cane growers in the state. This price is called as State Advisory Price. The State Government's policy in cane price fixing is to encourage the sugarcane cultivation and sugar production. The sugar price is fixed as per the regulations of Central Government and State Government has not to play any role in this regard. To sum up, almost all aspects of sugar industry are controlled by Central and State Governments in view of the welfare of farmers and consumers. The controls are meaningfully excercised as to enable industry and farmer to develop.

Significance of Co-operative Sugar Industry

The establishment of large modern factory may directly and indirectly assist the development of the region in which the factory is located. Co-operative sugar factories take a lead in economic development of the region[16]. The Indian economy is basically an agrarian economy. The incentive to agricultural development is a fair return to farmers, which can be given only after the development of agro-based industries like co-operative sugar factories. Agro-based industries like co-operative sugar factories have a large potential of creating employment in the rural area. Agro-based industries in rural areas help in dispersal of industries and ultimately for balanced regional development. Co-operative sugar factories play a very important role in this regard. The co-operative form of agro-based industry like sugar factory is more beneficial as the people in the rural area can have their own contribution in industrial development and they can have the fruits of economic development. The experience of co-operative sugar factories in Maharashtra has proved that the agricultural processing units in co-operative sector, if managed well, can provide a very good scope for rural development[17]. The sugar factories, being large size agro processing industry, has got quite a good employment potential. A sugar factory of 2500 TCD capacity creates an employment of around 500 permanent workers and 400 seasonal workers. In addition, in crushing season it provides employment to about 10,000 male and female workers for harvesting, 2000 bullock carts and about 200 trucks and tractors are used for transportation which provide employment to around 5000 workers. On an average, a co-operative sugar factory of 2500 TCD capacity creates employment to about 22000 to 25000 people in its area.

Sugar industry in Maharashtra have certain special benefits of co-operative form it has adopted. Co-operative sugar factories, besides creating employment potentialities, have provided the avenues of socio-economic development of their members and neighbouring areas. The co-operative sugar factories have provided an opportunity to even marginal cane-growers to derive the benefit of large scale industry. The co-operative sugar factories with their manifold advantages, play a very crucial role in bringing out socio-economic development of the rural areas. Almost all sugar factories in Maharashtra have undertaken several activities for social, agricultural, educational, cultural and economic development in their area of operation. Various activities have been undertaken by the co-operative sugar factories for rural development.

Need and Significance of the Study

The experience in co-operative sugar factories in Maharashtra has proved that the agricultural processing units in co-operative sector, if managed well, can provide a good scope for rural development. The co-operative sugar factories in Maharashtra are playing a role of catalyst in the process of socio-economic development of rural areas. Maharashtra is pioneering state in co-operative sugar industry in India. It has made admirable and noteworthy progress in sugar industry in co-operative sector.

In spite of this success the co-operative sugar industry in Maharashtra is facing various problems and has become a centre of criticism due to several reasons. It has been a common observation that co-operative sugar factories in the state are lagging behind in management efficiency. They are not able to control their costs, hence major co-operative sugar factories in the state and particularly in Marathwada region are carrying huge losses. The experts in this field attribute these losses to several factors like short supply of quality sugarcane, under utilisation of capacity, low sugar recovery rate, shortage of funds and inefficient management. It should be noted that working capital deficit is stated as the common problem of all factories. The fact is adequate working capital finance is provided to every co-operative sugar factory. State government do not hesitate in providing finance considering the role of co-operative sugar factories in rural economic development. In spite of encouraging policy and strong financial support of State Government, major co-operative sugar factories in the state are carrying huge losses since several years. This implies that the problem lies in management. This reveals that not the shortage but the mismanagement of working capital is the real problem, that led co-operative sugar factories to losses. Considering the significance of working capital management in maintaining profitability and financial strength and equally considering the significant role of co-operative sugar factories in the economic life of rural Marathwada region of the Maharashtra state, the problem entitled 'management of working capital in sugar co-operatives' with reference to Marathwada region is undertaken for detailed study. It is expected that the study will be helpful in understanding the working capital problems and in finding solutions. In this respect the study is significant and useful.

Objective of the Study

The present study is designed to examine management of working capital in sugar co-operatives in Marathwada region of Maharashtra state. Following are the specific objective of the study:

(i) To examine the working capital trends and liquidity of working capital in co-operative sugar factories in Marathwada region.

(ii) To evaluate Inventory management in co-operative sugar factories in Marathwada region.

(iii) To analyse receivable management in co-operative sugar factories in Marathwada.

(iv) To examine the cash management practice in co-operative sugar factories in Marathwada.

Period of Study

To be more precise in analysis it was necessary to define the period of study. The study period is taken as ten years from 1991-92 to 2000-01. These are the financial years of co-operative sugar factories, commencing 1st April and ending on 31st March every year. The period of ten years is quite enough to determine the trend of working capital and to examine the problem of management of working capital.

Sample Design

The present study pertains to Marathwada region of Maharashtra State. At present 36 co-operative sugar factories are operating in Marathwada region. Fourteen co-operative sugar factories of Marathwada region are selected for study. The units are selected on the district basis, i.e. two from each district. The districts are Aurangabad, Jalna, Beed, Parbhani, Nanded, Latur and Osmanabad. While taking samples only those factories were considered for study which were continuously in operation during the study period. An attempt was made to select sample factories with the two types of crushing capacities, i.e. 1250 TCD per day and 2500 TCD per day. The list of sugar factories selected for study is as follows:

List of Sugar Factories Selected for the Study

	Name of the Factories and District	*Crushing Capacity in TCD*
	Aurangabad:	
1.	Shri Sant Eknath SSK. Ltd. Eknathnagar, Paithan	1250
2.	Siddheshwar SSK. Ltd. Maniknagar, Sillod.	2500
	Jalna:	
1.	Jalna SSK. Ltd. Ramnagar, Jalna	1250
2.	Samarth SSK. Ltd., Ankushnagar, Ambad	2500
	Beed:	
1.	Shri Gajanan SSK Ltd., Rajuri, Beed	1250
2.	Jai Bhavani SSK Ltd., Shivajinagar, Georai	2500
	Parbhani:	
1.	Godavari Dudhna SSK. Ltd., Pathri	1250
2.	Purna SSK. Ltd., Vasmatnagar, Wasmat	2500
	Nanded:	
1.	Shankar SSK Ltd., Waghalwada, Bhokar	1250
2.	Godavari Manar, Shankarnagar, Billoli	2500
	Latur:	
1.	Jai Jawan Jai Kisan, Nalegaon, Chakur	1250
2.	Manjra SSK Ltd., Vilasnagar, Latur	2500
	Osmanabad:	
1.	Tuljabhavani SSK Ltd., Tuljapur	1250
2.	Terna SSK Ltd., Dhoki, Osmanabad	2500

Research Methodology

The present study management of working capital in sugar co-operatives in Marathwada region is based on secondary data. Marathwada region of Maharashtra State is famous for co-operative movement particularly in sugar industry. There are 36 co-operative sugar factories in Marathwada region but only 14 co-operative sugar factories are selected as sample for the study. The data was collected from sample sugar factories mainly through annual reports for the study period of ten years, i.e. from 1991-92 to 2000-01. Some data are also collected from the Office of the Regional Joint Director (Sugar) Aurangabad and Nanded. Data related to sugar factories are also collected from the books, journals and periodicals, such as Indian Sugar, Co-operative Sugar and Annual reports of Maharastra Rajya Sahakari Sakhar Karkhana Sangh, etc.

The data so collected were tabulated and comparisons were made on the basis of growth indices, average and percentage. Some ratios are used for analysis of working capital. The ratio mainly used are working capital, turnover ratio, current ratio, quick ratio, inventory turnover ratio and receivable turnover ratio, etc.

Scope and Limitations of the Study

While considering research on a particular area of the vast field of financial management, a researcher has to face certain difficulties which put limitations on research work. Following are the limitations of the study.

1. The study limited to fourteen sugar factories as sample from all over Marathwada region of Maharashtra State. Only co-operative sugar factories are studied. Sugar factories other than in co-operative sector are not considered.
2. The sample factories chosen are those which were in operation during the study period. The factories which were not in regular operation during study period were not considered for sample.
3. The analysis is based on the data published in annual reports of the selected co-operative sugar factories.
4. The effect of inflation on working capital and its components are not considered. There were not much fluctuations in the price levels of items. The data of price level changes could not be made available. Thus effect of inflation is not considered.

Scheme of Chapters

The present book is divided into eight chapters. The first chapter deals with introduction, historical background, development of sugar industry in India, Maharashtra and Marathwada. It also gives the objective of the present study, research methodology and scheme of chapters.

The second chapter is devoted to review the relevant and recent literature on the sugar industry and working capital management in sugar co-operatives.

The third chapter deals with the profile of co-operative sugar factories selected under study. It gives detailed information of the co-operative sugar factories and development programmes undertaken by factories under study.

The fourth chapter presents the working capital management trends and liquidity analysis. It examines the types of working capital, structure of working capital, working capital trends and working capital turnover ratio in co-operative sugar factories. It also deals with the liquidity analysis. Current ratio and quick ratio are also calculated.

Fifth chapter discusses the inventory management. It analyses the need to hold inventories, functions of inventory management and inventory management in co-operative sugar factories. The chapter analyses in brief the growth of inventories, inventory turnover ratio and control over inventories.

Sixth chapter deals with the receivables management. It discusses the nature and objectives of receivables, growth of receivables, account receivable turnover ratio and control over receivables. The chapter ends with conclusions.

Seventh chapter deals with cash management. This chapter deliberate on objectives of holding cash and functions of cash management. It discusses the cash inflows and outflows, the organisation of cash management, growth of cash, control over cash, cash to sales ratio, cash to working capital ratio etc.

The eighth and final chapter summarises the conclusions of the present study and suggests policy measures, based on the conclusions, to improve the efficiency of working capital management in co-operative sugar factories.

REFERENCES

1. Jain A.P., Foreword to Grower's Own Co-opretive Sugar Factories, Ministry of Food and Agriculture, Govt. of India, New Dehli, 1956. p. 10.
2. Inamdar (Indamar) N.R., Govt. and Co-operative Sugar Factories, Popular Publication, Bombay, 1965. p. 1 & 2.
3. Bapat N.G., Economic Development of Ahmednagar District 1880-1960. Progressive Corporation Pvt. Ltd., Bombay, 1973. p. 312.

4. Shrishrimal W.S. The Mechanism of Determining Cane Price in Co-operative Sugar Factories in Maharashtra, The Maharashtra Co-operative Qtr., Vol. No. 4, April 1967. p. 89.

5. Mohite Y.J., Sugarcane Industry of Maharashtra (Blueprint of Progress) Govt. of Maharashtra, Bombay, 1974. p. 3.

6. Shrishrimal W.C., Ibid. pp. 49-52.

7. Vasantdada Sugar Institute, Pune. As quoted By Miss. Sangeeta R. Kurulkar "Location Patterns of Sugar Industry in Maharashtra" Ph.D. unpublished Thesis Dr. BAMU, A. Bad.

8. *Ibid.*

9. G. Gour, Co-operative Sugar—January 1999. p. 410.

10. R.M. Kharche, Industrial Development of Maharashtra, Chamber of Commerce and Industry, Pune, 1987. p. 85.

11. R.M. Kharche, op. cit. p. 134.

12. P.J. Manoharrao, Bhartiya Sugar Directory—1987. p. 9.

13. Kuralkar Sangeeta, op. cit. p. 57.

2

Review of Literature

India was importing sugar to meet the consumers needs of the country till 1957. Thereafter sugar industry in India has become one of the important foreign exchange earning industries. The Government of India has taken various measures for its proper growth and development. The government adopted industrial policy, which resulted in setting up of large number of sugar factories in private as well as co-operative sector. The industrial policy resolution of 1956 has given preference to the setting up of co-operative sugar factories. Accordingly, right from the first five-year plan emphasis was given on promoting the co-operative movement, for bringing in the socialistic pattern of society, which is the ultimate objective of planning in this country. With the growing up of the industry large number of problems were noticed by the sugar industry itself and by the government in particulars. The problems of sugar industry were manifold such as the problems of finance, availability of raw material, problem relating to management, problem relating to labourers, etc. The Government of India appointed various committees from time to time to study the problems of sugar industry and make suggestions for its improvement. Like- wise the state government also appointed various committees to study the problems of sugar industry and make recommendations to government for taking policy decisions.

Besides, various researchers and scholars have made efforts to study the sugar industry from its different angles. The growth of sugar industry in India has helped the economy in many ways. The co-operative sugar factories have played pivotal role in modernisation of agriculture, socio-economic and educational transformation of rural society.

It has already been pointed out that the sugar industry is the second largest agro-based industry in India. It is situated in the rural areas and considering the highly perishable nature of the raw material, i.e. sugarcane, this industry leaves a deep impact on rural economy. With the development in agriculture, it was felt necessary to start and promote ancillary industries which not only convert the agriculture goods into finished products but also increase their value.

Taking into account the importance of sugar industry in national economy a number of researchers have worked on the various aspects of sugar industry such as development and problems of the sugar industry and its prospects. Similarly, government policy and regional planning for sugar industry area, labour situation in the industry, the lives of farmers and agriculture labourers, the financial management of sugar industry, the importance of sugar co-operatives in rural economy and such other aspects of the industry also have been probed into. In this chapter an attempt has been made to review the studies conducted on sugar co-operatives in India after independence.

Dr. G.S. Kamath[1] has studied the management of co-operative enterprise with special reference to sugar co-operative in Maharashtra and published his work in 1965. He studied problems relating to finance, raw material, personnel of co-operative sugar factories, their management and their role in rural development.

Roy Choudhary[2] had undertaken a study with a view to observe the problems of the co-operative sugar factories. The results of the study showed that the sugar factories are not only intended for processing sugarcane mainly for sugar but also for a number of by products. They have no other use, therefore, solely dependent on sugarcane supplied. Sugarcane constitutes the major portion in the total cost of sugar production.

Andhale G.B.[3] studied the impact of co-operative sugar factories on the lives of the farmers with special reference to Sangmaner Bhag Sahakari Sakhar Karkhana Ltd., Sangmaner in Ahmednagar district in 1972. He has restricted his work to the impact of sugar factory on the sugarcane producing members of the factory. But it is also clear that non-shareholders are equally important in supplying cane to the factory.

Choudhary's[4] study in 1974 pertains to a case of one sugar factory in Maharashtra. He studied the management of working capital, its deficiencies, requirements and suggested a few possible causes which could be attributed to bad financial management, such as payment of outstanding interest and dividends, operating losses, current funds used to add to fixed assets, i.e. diversion of short term resources to finance long term investments, reduction of stocks and bonds, i.e. refund of shares, an expanded volume of business and current assets that required more working capital than was available. Moreover, redemption of long term debts was made out of current resources. He evaluated the cash cycle using current ratio to manage working capital. Secondly, he prepared the fund flow analysis of working capital for two years (1970 and 1971) through comparative balance sheet and statement of variations of capital. The projection of working capital requirements was done for two years. The computation of working capital was also done for two years. The computations of working capital requirements were done by preparing the projected expenses for the said period.

In this study, the author has observed the deficiencies in working capital due to occasional investments, expansion and repayments of long term loan etc. without causing financial embarrassment. The study of working capital was based on average recovery of sugar. It concluded with a note that "the factory may not have any difficulty in its requirements of working capital".

According to Kharkar[5], now a days though there is an emphasis on increasing production capacity of the factory, it leads to push the factory into losses due to under utilisation of the capacity. The economics of scale are therefore, too obvious to be emphasized in any processing industry. Kharkar has specifically pointed out that economics of sugar factory is distributed largely because of low productivity and crushing of sugarcane of nonshareholders who produce the cane of poor quality. This statement, however, seems to be particularly invalid for the reason that the recovery percentage of sources of sugarcane to factory was quite encouraging.

In 1976 N.S. Jain[6] worked on the "Regional Economic Planning in Sugar Factory Area". Jain has selected the area of their co-operative sugar factory at Haveli taluka in Pune district. According to him, the area has not been developed with due consideration of the requirements of the modern technique of regional planning and needs of the region. Jain has attempted to study the proper demarcation of functions between the sugar factories and other local planning agencies and to determine the propriety of entrusting particular planning functions to an organisation like co-operative sugar factory. Apart from this, he has also considered the problems of sugar industry and reference is made to the important aspects of the impact at the micro level, such as impact on irrigation facilities, agricultural development, employment in rural area, etc. But the impact on farmers, industrial and agricultural labour, non-agricultural trade and commerce, transport and communication etc. are not studied.

Haldaye D.G.[7] attempted a study on workers participation in sugar industry and added few points in favour of ideal industrial democracy, social objectives, right of workers etc. He referred the co-operative sugar factories in Haryana where the entire employees are shareholders. It was being discussed since 1965 with both national and state federations of co-operative sugar factories. The Government of Maharashtra appointed a committee under the guidance of Dhanajayrao Gadgil to workout manner in which workers could be made shareholder. The then Union Food and Agriculture Minister, Jagjeevan Ram supported the idea of making employees shareholders, to improve the financial strength and create the work culture.

Kharche[8] studied the cane development programme in sugar factory areas with special reference to sick factories and found that the low production of sugarcane in factory areas was due to:

1. Inadequate staff for implementation of sugarcane development scheme;
2. Lack of arrangements for hot water treatment and the mercuric compound treatment to seeds;
3. Untimely availability of finances;
4. Primitive method of cultivation of sugarcane; and
5. Inability of the sick units to pay even minimum cane price.

These entire factors together limit the supply of cane to the factories, which results in very poor crushing and still more losses.

Shah and Shah[9] pointed out that the cost of production of sugar factory depends primarily on the raw material, the sugar recovery percentage and the duration of crushing season. They suggested that the cost of sugar production could be brought down by utilising the processing unit for a maximum period and by proper checking of the machinery of its day-to-day work. The cost of extra fuel, lubricants, spare parts, consumption of chemicals and sugar content in final molasses could be reduced, if the steam balance and machinery are maintained.

Tupe,[10] in his work 'Impact of Sugar Factories on the Rural Economy', A case study has been done on the impact of Sanjivani Co-operative Sugar Factory in Ahmednagar district on agriculture, agriculturist, on the lives of agriculture labour, economic conditions of factory worker and spared effects of the sugar factory and overall economic change in rural area. He concluded with the findings that sugarcane being cash crop, area under sugarcane has increased, the area under irrigation has increased and likewise the changes in the cropping pattern and methods of farming have changed. It is argued that the development of agriculture depends on major agro-based industries. The real income of the farmers has increased but the real income of the agriculture labourers has been decreased. It is concluded by the author that the sugar factory in rural area has worked as growth center.

B.S. Baviskar[11] submitted his Ph.D. thesis on "The politics of Development of Sugar Co-operative in Rural Maharashtra" in 1980. In his thesis he made detail study of Kisan Co-operative Sugar Factory, Kopargaon, district Ahmednagar. He studied the factors which are necessary to successful running of the factory. He evaluated the success and advantages of the sugar factory and he analysed the interrelation between co-operative movement and politics. In his study he observed that in rural Maharashtra the nature and system of politics.

The Government of Maharashtra[12] appointed a committee for studying the problems of sick co-operative sugar factories under the chairmanship of Shri Gulabrao Patil. The committee found that inadequate supply of sugarcane, lack of sugarcane increase in the project cost and lack of term loan arrangements, associated with relatively lower equity and excess burden of interest on short-term loans, lack of experienced technical personnel for efficient use of machinery, inefficient management and lack of long-term price policy for sugarcane, were the major reasons for sustained losses in sugar production.

Jagdishlal and Bajpai's[13] study was indicated that growth rate of sugarcane production was highest in Tamilnadu followed by Karnataka, Maharashtra, Punjab, Uttar Pradesh, Andhra Pradesh and Bihar. Most of the tropical states had growth rate of area, production and prices, higher than those of sub-tropical states. The states having high growth rates of cane or Gur prices also had higher growth rates of area and production. In the state with higher growth rates of area or production, the availability in area, production, productivity and price were observed to be higher in the states having higher growth rates of these variables. They have said that it is desirable to bring about substantial improvement in productivity for which efforts should be made for replacement of currently grown varieties with superior ones, timely and adequate supply of strategic inputs, effective transfer of plant and modern sugarcane technology, control of disease and pests, drainage for water logged areas, reclamation of saline alkali soils and timely payments of cane price to farmers.

Sood H.C.[14] studied modernisation of Indian sugar industry. He has stated that, the year 1987-88 was remained historic with the record cane production, around 180 million tons, and sugar production of 9.1 million tons, surpassing the sugar production in Cuba and Brazil. He emphasized on full capacity utilisation, ensuring considerable export and profitability to the industry. He urged that factories should encash efforts taken by National Sugar Institute of Kanpur, Deccan Sugar Institute Pune and National Federation of Co-operative Sugar Factories for the betterment of sugar industry. He has supported the idea of capacity expansion.

Tyagrajan R.V.[15] discussed the problems and prospects of sugar industry and stated that traditionally sugar production has been subject to fluctuations, i.e. sugar cycle ranging from 4 to 5 years and a pragmatic sugar policy initiated by Government since 1985-86, has resulted in increasing the sugar production. He also stated that yield of cane per acre has declined precipitously about 15% to 20% in most part of the country.

He expressed that while sugar industry is controlled by Government alternate sweetners enjoy complete freedom from centre and they can sell entire production in open market, resulting in diversion of cane to Khandsari and Gur production. He also observed price indices for all commodities together for the period of 1973-74 to 1989-90, moved by 15% p.a. against 9.4% for sugar, 17.2% for pulses and 11% for wheat.

Dr. Nikam G.A.[16] has made financial and cost analysis of sugar co-operatives in Maharashtra. The study covers 9 co-operative sugar factories of the state. The study deals with the composition of various cost components and their magnitude in the total cost of sugar production. It also aims to find out the changes that have taken place over a given period of time and to judge profitability and financial strength of the sugar factories under study. The performance of these 9 co-operative sugar factories is measured and conclusions are drawn. They may certainly provide guidelines to managements, government and shareholders. The study deals with cost trends, profitability and financial strength. The study concludes with the need of control over cost, need of special costing department in sugar factories, need of sugar cane development and need of training to management personnel.

B. Ramchandra Reddey[17] published a book "Financial Management in Co-operatives". In his book he selected three co-operative sugar factories from the State of Tamilnadu for detailed study. He examined in detail the capital structure and cost of capital, capital budget, working capital management, distribution of surplus, financial management in co-operatives, etc. He recommends the following suggestions:

1. It is found that the Government interferes in the functioning of co-operative sugar factories. The co-operative sugar factories should be free to work by democratic system.
2. There is need to increase internal sources of capital.
3. The co-operative sugar factories may have to pay the interest on capital of shareholder so as to increase the amount of share capital.
4. Sugar factories should pay the sugarcane price promptly.
5. To improve the efficiency of workers there is need for training and orientation programmes for them.
6. Sugar development programme should be implemented in sugar factories. To avoid the shortage of sugarcane proper planning of sugarcane is needed.
7. The repairs of machinery and use of by products may be done in off-season of the sugar factory. In the interest of the factory and the shareholder there may be planned development programme.

Narasaiah A., and Jaychandra A.,[18] attempted a study on cash management in co-operative sugar factories. Being a case study and its influence on liquidity, they expressed that sugar industry has not only developed rural area but also acted as largest contributor to state and central exchequer, however, financial performance of many sugar factories was not seen satisfactory.

They also observed that the factory maintained lower current ratio than standard ratio of 2:1, expressing, inability to cover current liabilities similarly, quick ratio also observed lower than standard ratio of 1:1 and expressed that high portion of cash improves the liquidity position.

Haridas K.E.[19] discussed the problems of Co-operative sugar industry and expressed that the Government has accepted policies in favour of co-operative sector to create socialistic pattern of society. He observed that both the regions, Marathwada and Vidharbha, are trailing in cane yielding and sugar recovery. He stated that sugar industry not only helps the progress of their members and employees but also helps agriculture labour, artisans and small businessmen. He also concentrated on cane development and capacity utilisation.

Desai Ashok V.,[20] indicated in his study, that Indian sugar industry is much cheap because of low cost of agriculture. However, the industry loses the benefits because of heavy factory cost, as small sized units and inefficient workings.

He also observed that the managements of sugar co-operatives have neither repaid the principal nor interest on loan. Average sugar price is also observed cheap, i.e. Rs. 12 per Kg. in 1995, as compared to Rs. 15 in Brazil, Rs. 21 in Australia, Rs. 22 in China, Rs. 33 in Germany and Rs. 66 in Japan.

Gohil Daxa,[21] studied the profitability in Bardoli co-operative sugar mill, based on the net profit, operating ratio, etc. She concluded that Asia's largest enterprise in terms of crushing capacity is suffering from the benefit because of low profitability. She suggested prudent measures of controlling over-head expenses ensuring effective utilization of available resources.

She also pointed that Government should nurture this industry, since it plays an important role in socio-economic development of the society.

Thus, various scholars have studied the different aspects of the sugar industry separately. It should be emphasized here that wherever a particular factory is established in a region, it influences the economy of the region from all the angles. Hence it would be better to take into consideration the impact of a factory as a whole and not by parts. The fast growth of the sugar industry has created number of problems regarding finance, cane availability etc. to the management of the sugar industry itself and to the state Government also. Hence, both the Central and State Governments have appointed several committees from time to time to resolve the problems.

Taking into account the importance of sugar industry in the national economy, number of research scholars, authors, scientists, prominent leaders, etc. have studied different aspects of the sugar industry.

In the present study, in addition to these aspects already mentioned, attempt has been made to study the management of working capital in sugar co-operatives in Marathwada region.

REFERENCES

1. Kamath G.S., —Management of Co-operative Enterprise with Special Reference to Sugar Co-operatives in Maharashtra, Ph.D. Thesis, Pune University, 1965.
2. Roy Choudhary., —Problems of the Co-operative Sugar Factories, Indian Co-operative Review, 1972, p. 23.
3. Anadhale G.B., —A Study of the Impact of a Co-operative Sugar Factory on the Lives of Farmers, B.Sc. (Agri.) Thesis, Mahatma Phule Krishi Vidyapeeth, Rahuri, 1972.
4. B.N. Choudhary., —Management of Sugar Industry with Special Reference to Co-operatives, Published in a Book Management of Sugar Industry, by Management Development Institute, New Delhi, First Publication, 1974.
5. Kharkar N.C., —Technological Evaluation of Sugar Factories in Maharashtra, Deccan Sugar Technologists Association, Pune, 1975, p. 15.
6. Jain N.S., —Regional Economic Planning in a Sugar Factory Area, Ph.D. Thesis, University of Poona, 1976.
7. Haldaye D.G. —Workers Participation in Sugar Industry, Maharashtra Sugar, 1977, p. 23.
8. Kharche, —A Co-operative Sugar Industry in Marathwada, Lead Industry for Development, Reference to Sick Factories from Marathwada and Vidarbha, 2(5), 1977, p. 15.
9. Shah H.P., and Shah N.K. —Measures for Reduction in Cost of Production of Sugar, Gujarat Association for Agricultural Science, 1980.
10. Tupe S.D., —The Impact of Sugar Factories on the Rural Economy—A Case Study, Ph.D Thesis, University of Poona, 1980.

11. B.S. Baviskar —The Politics of Development of Sugar Co-operative in Rural Maharashtra, Unpublished Thesis, Pune University, Pune, 1980.
12. Government of Maharashtra Sugarcane Control Order by Government of Maharashtra, dated 28th March, 1985.
13. Jagdish Lal and R.K. Bajpai, —Measuring Growth in Area, Production, Productivity and Prices of Sugarcane and Its Competing Crops and Gur in India, Bhartiya Sugar, 11(9), 1986.
14. Sood H.C., —Modernisation of Indian Sugar Industry, Bhartiya Sugar, 1989, p. 27.
15. Tyagrajan R.V. 1986, —Problem and Prospects of Sugar Industry, Indian Sugar, Sept. 1981, p. 339.
16. Dr. Nikam G.A., —Financial and Cost Analysis, Sugar Co-operative, Indu Prakashan , Pune, 1991.
17. B. Ramchandra, —Financial Management in Co-operatives, Printwell Publication, Jaipur.
18. Singh K.V. Malik, Sanjeev Kumar and Lal Jagdish, —Inter-Regional Trend Analysis of Sugarcane Acreage, Production and Productivity in Uttar Pradesh, Agricultural Situation in India, Vol. XI IX, No. 3 May, 1994.
19. Haridas K.E. —Problem of Co-operative Sugar Industry Gramved, K.B. Rohamare, Smruti Granth Prakashan, Kopargaon, 1998, p. 121.
20. Desai Ashok V, —Our Tooth, Indian Sugar, Jan. 1999, p. 825.
21. Gohil Daxa, —Profitability in Bardoli Co-operative Sugar Mill, Co-operative Sugar, March 2000, p. 541.

3

Profile of Sugar Factories in Marathwada

Introduction

In earlier chapter we have taken a general review of the sugar industry in India and more particularly co-operative sugar factories in Maharashtra. The co-operative sector in sugar factories came up during the first five year plan and with subsequent five year plans more and more licenses have been issued to co-operative sugar factories. The policy of the Government of India showed a shift from private sector to co-operative sector. The private sector always keeps before it the objective of profit while in the co-operative sector the emphasis is on the welfare of the farmers who produce sugarcane. Of course, the motive of earning profit can never be discarded. Today the sugar co-operatives are playing vital role in the rural economy of the state.

The present study is a study of selected factories in Marathwada. For micro purpose, fourteen co-operative sugar factories were selected as sample from Marathwada region, i.e. two from each district. The factories have been selected from each district on the basis of their crushing capacity, i.e. (1) 1250 TCD and (2) 2500 TCD and above. Following co-operative sugar factories were included in the study.

1. Aurangabad District

(a) Shri Sant Eknath SSK Ltd., Eknathnagar, Paithan

(b) Siddheshwar SSK Ltd., Maniknagar, Sillod

2. Jalna District

(a) Jalna SSK Ltd., Ramnagar, Jalna

(b) Samarth SSK Ltd., Ankushnagar, Ambad

3. Beed District

(a) Gajanan SSK Ltd., Rajuri, Beed

(b) Jaibhavani SSK Ltd., Shivajinagar, Georai

4. Parbhani District

(a) Godawari Dudhana SSK Ltd., Pathri

(b) Purna SSK Ltd., Wasmatnagar, Wasmat

5. Nanded District

(a) Shankar SSK Ltd., Wagalwada, Bhokar

(b) Godawari Manar SSK Ltd., Shankarnagar, Biloli

6. Latur District

(a) Jai Jawan Jai Kisan SSK Ltd., L.B. Shatrinagar, Tq. Chakur.

(b) Manjra SSK Ltd., Vilasnagar, Latur

7. Osmanabad District

(a) Tuljabhavani SSK Ltd., Tuljapur

(b) Terna SSK Ltd., Ternanagar, Osmanabad

AURANGABAD DISTRICT

Following two factories were selected for study from Aurangabad district.

(a) Shri Sant Eknath SSK Ltd., Paithan

(b) Siddheshwar SSK Ltd., Maniknagar, Sillod

(a) Shri Sant Eknath SSK Ltd., Paithan

Shri Sant Eknath SSK Ltd. was registered in 1971 with a production capacity of 1250 TCD. At present crushing capacity of the factory is 1250 TCD. The factory covers the area of Paithan Taluka. The number of villages covered under the area of operation is 140. The operational details of the factory are as follows[1]:

Table—3.1: Sugar Production (1991-92 to 2000-01)

Year	*Sugarcane Crushed M.T.*	*Sugar Produced (Quintel)*	*Recovery (%)*	*Gross Working Days*	*Final Price Paid to Growers P.T.*
1991-92	237904	268020	10.06	170	332
1992-93	137958	157360	11.16	129	368
1993-94	Close	Close	Close	Close	Close
1994-95	207788	218835	10.53	156	565
1995-96	228784	221000	9.59	195	460
1996-97	77194	78560	9.65	112	460
1997-98	Close	Close	Close	Close	Close
1998-99	160436	160650	10.47	149	607
1999-2000	288154	335405	11.22	189	643
2000-2001	235870	268640	11.40	155	709

Development Programmes

The factory had planned development programme in plantation. The seeding of different varieties was planned in different specified areas allotted to each variety. This method had ensured matured sugarcane supply throughout the extended season. Sugarcane development programme of the factory has been set up to achieve one particular objective and that is to raise the recovery rate of sugarcane. It is clear from the above table that factory has been more or less successful in achieving the goal. The recovery rate has been satisfactory. This achievement was possible when various schemes are planned and implemented successfully. The schemes planned can briefly be stated as under.

1. Supply of Fertilizer

The factory supplies compost manures and chemical fertilizers to the sugarcane growers. The sugarcane yield and the recovery rate mostly depend on the use of manures and fertilizers. These inputs are required for the growth of sugarcane.

2. Competition for Higher Sugarcane Production

The factory planned rewards for sugarcane growers. The factory decided to constitute rewards for highest producer of sugarcane, which shows a high rate of recovery for the season 2000-01. This scheme helpd to create a competitive spirit among the sugarcane growers.

(b) Siddheshwar SSK Ltd., Maniknagar, Sillod

Siddheshwar SSK Ltd. was registered in 1970. The production capacity at the time of commencement was 1250 TCD and now it is 2000 TCD. The factory covers an area of two talukas those are Bhokardan and Sillod. Bhokardan belongs to Jalna District. The number of villages covered by area of operation is 166. The operational details are as follows[2].

Table—3.2: Sugar Production (1991-92 to 2000-01)

Year	*Sugarcane Crushed M.T.*	*Sugar Produced (Quintel)*	*Recovery (%)*	*Gross Working Days*	*Final Price Paid to Growers P.T.*
1991-92	353166	370291	10.47	195	400
1992-93	163139	158455	9.71	113	525
1993-94	265336	267021	10.06	144	750
1994-95	430728	432775	10.06	199	675
1995-96	323955	343900	10.59	153	628
1996-97	163149	173780	10.61	110	600
1997-98	Close	Close	Close	Close	Close
1998-99	339441	334210	9.70	201	670
1999-2000	375033	398760	10.63	176	800
2000-2001	254813	270520	10.61	139	800

Development Programmes

It is observed that the factory has planned and implemented the sugarcane development programme. The factory provides improved sugarcane seeds to the farmers. The new varieties of sugarcane seeds, i.e. Co-C-671 and CO86032, 8014, planted for the benefit of the farmers.

Factory provides educational facilities to children of members, cane growers and staff of the factory. Factory has established an industrial training institute to impart technical education to the students by the institute.

JALNA DISTRICT

Following two factories were selected for study from Jalna district:

(a) Jalna SSK Ltd., Ramnagar, Jalna.

(b) Samarth SSK Ltd., Ankushnagar, Ambad.

(a) Jalna SSK Ltd. Ramnagar, Jalna

Jalna SSK Ltd. registered in 1984 and started its production in 1987 with production capacity of 1250 TCD. At present crushing capacity of the factory is 1250 TCD. The number of villages covered by the area of operation is 243. The operational details of the factory are as follows.[3]

Table—3.3: Sugar Production (1991-92 to 2000-01)

Year	*Sugarcane Crushed M.T.*	*Sugar Produced (Quintel)*	*Recovery (%)*	*Gross Working Days*	*Final Price Paid to Growers P.T.*
1991-92	323661	337930	10.44	184	455
1992-93	236764	247965	10.47	163	491
1993-94	236073	237775	10.00	150	701
1994-95	304013	281785	9.27	215	561
1995-96	219508	203901	9.68	190	460
1996-97	Close	Close	Close	Close	Close
1997-98	Close	Close	Close	Close	Close
1998-99	140573	141620	9.78	159	567
1999-2000	224775	216512	9.63	181	565
2000-2001	104864	102785	9.80	131	580

Development Programmes

Area development activities undertaken by factory include development of cane seed and distribution of fertilizer. Factory provided fertilizer to the cane growers and supplied cane seed to shareholder members. Educational and health facilities are given by the factory to the family of the staff.

The factory provides educational facilities to the children of members and sugarcane growers and staff of the factory.

(b) Samarth SSK Ltd., Ankushnagar, Ambad

Samarth SSK Ltd. was registered in 1982. The production capacity at the time of commencement was 1250 TCD. Production capacity was expanded in 1989 to 2500 TCD. The factory covers an area of two Talukas of Jalna district Ambad and Ghansavangi. The number of villages covered by area of operation are 253. The operational details of the factory are as follows[4]:

Table—3.4: Sugar Production (1991-92 to 2000-01)

Year	*Sugarcane Crushed M.T.*	*Sugar Produced (Quintel)*	*Recovery (%)*	*Gross Working Days*	*Final Price Paid to Growers P.T.*
1991-92	280189	300915	10.72	185	375
1992-93	178591	197210	11.02	135	400
1993-94	93003	94465	10.08	94	556
1994-95	362961	375430	10.33	220	672
1995-96	473236	500080	10.55	221	595
1996-97	193846	206040	10.60	130	610
1997-98	189419	198160	10.34	144	648
1998-99	393807	439188	11.13	178	718
1999-2000	604374	668912	11.06	245	800
2000-2001	476412	564890	11.85	177	850

Development Programmes

The development programmes of this factory has been aimed to achieve one particular objective and that is to raise the recovery rate of sugarcane. It can be seen from the table given above, that the factory has been more or less successful in achieving the targets. The recovery rate was consistently higher than 10.08%. This achievement can only be possible when various schemes of development are planned and implemented successfully. The schemes planned out can briefly stated as given below:

1. Irrigation

The factory is lucky enough to be working under a zone irrigated by canal water. However, lift irrigation schemes are found to be necessary for land, which does not fall under Canal Zone. The factory planned to irrigate more and more land in the area of operation.

2. Supply of fertilizer

The factory supplies compost manures and chemical fertilizers to sugarcane growers. The sugarcane yield and the recovery rate mostly depend on the use of manures and fertilizers. The use of these inputs are required for growth of sugarcane.

BEED DISTRICT

Following two factories were selected for study from Beed district:

(a) Gajanan SSK Ltd., Rajuri, Tq. Beed

(b) Jai Bhavani SSK Ltd., Georai, Beed

(a) Gajanan SSK Ltd., Rajuri, Tq. Beed

Gajanan SSK Ltd. was registered in 1984 and started its work in the prime area of sugarcane crop in Beed Taluka, district Beed. The production capacity at the time of commencement was 1250 TCD and still it is 1250 TCD. The area of operation of this factory are four Talukas that are Beed, Wadvani, Patoda and Dharur. Other operational details of the factory for the period from 1991-92 to 2000-01 are as follows[5]:

Table—3.5: Sugar Production (1991-92 to 2000-01)

Year	*Sugarcane Crushed M.T.*	*Sugar Produced (Quintel)*	*Recovery (%)*	*Gross Working Days*	*Final Price Paid to Growers P.T.*
1991-92	145400	147645	10.10	119	307
1992-93	Close	Close	Close	Close	Close
1993-94	Close	Close	Close	Close	Close
1994-95	182420	181905	9.91	193	590
1995-96	149667	128520	8.50	204	460
1996-97	44351	38475	8.50	96	460
1997-98	Close	Close	Close	Close	Close
1998-99	127979	125500	9.67	136	667
1999-2000	218441	211685	9.55	196	567
2000-2001	231639	264700	10.60	155	658

Implementation of Sugarcane Development Programmes

No sugar factory can afford to neglect such schemes, which ensure reliable supply of sugarcane. Irrigation facility is very much necessary to the Gajanan Co-operative Sugar Factory preferably to promote the sugarcane grower to produce more and more sugarcane. Since most of the farmers are ignorant of the new developments and techniques in sugarcane production, the factory planned a programme of taking this knowledge to the doors of the grower. The factory developed their own plant nursery near by the factory. It provides free of charge cane plants for cane growers, members and staff of the factory. Besides this factory has decided to cultivate the improved seeds of sugar cane in their own farm.

(b) Jaibhavani SSK Ltd., Georai, Beed

Jaibhavani SSK Ltd. was registered in 1973 with a cane crushing capacity of 1250 TCD. The production capacity expanded in 1991 to 2500 TCD. The factory is working in two Talukas of Beed district that are Beed and Georai. The number of villages covered by area of operation is 197. The operational details of the factory are as follows[6]:

Table—3.6: Sugar Production (1991-92 to 2000-01)

Year	*Sugarcane Crushed M.T.*	*Sugar Produced (Quintel)*	*Recovery (%)*	*Gross Working Days*	*Final Price Paid to Growers P.T.*
1991-92	317893	334175	10.50	168	339.80
1992-93	139101	153805	11.11	129	359.50
1993-94	Close	Close	Close	Close	Close
1994-95	313390	325875	10.53	152	667
1995-96	375325	336780	8.95	226	460
1996-97	189473	208780	10.14	133	500
1997-98	193894	186171	9.59	156	708
1998-99	347439	300370	10.63	167	670
1999-2000	461708	484815	10.46	211	685
2000-2001	404706	440901	10.90	171	769

Objects and Activities

1. To manufacture sugar and allied products.
2. To achieve allround development of the area of operation.

The factory developed the following schemes:

(i) Bhavani Urban Co-op. Bank Ltd.

(ii) Godawari Co-op. Consumer society

(iii) Jai Bhavani educational institute.

PARBHANI DISTRICT

Parbhani district is now divided into two districts, i.e. Hingoli and Parbhani. Following two factories are selected for study from old Parbhani district.

(a) Godawari Dudhana SSK Ltd., Pathri

(b) Purna SSK Ltd., Wasmatnagar, Wasmat

(a) Godawari Dudhana SSK Ltd., Pathri

Godawari Dudhana SSK Ltd. was registered in 1975 with production capacity of 1250 TCD. At present crushing capacity of the factory is 1250 TCD. The factory covers an area of five Talukas that are Pathri, Jintoor, Parbhani, Majalgaon and Partur. The number of villages covered by area of operation is 139. The operational details of the factory are as follows[7]:

Table—3.7: Sugar Production (1991-92 to 2000-01)

Year	*Sugarcane Crushed M.T.*	*Sugar Produced (Quintel)*	*Recovery (%)*	*Gross Working Days*	*Final Price Paid to Growers P.T.*
1991-92	262428	290451	11.04	188	368
1992-93	195276	218853	11.17	140	460
1993-94	115521	126382	10.57	225	600
1994-95	318548	334545	10.48	201	624
1995-96	237201	234068	9.87	104	460
1996-97	69844	64070	9.16	85	460
1997-98	40841	38062	8.90	94	640
1998-99	85500	89075	10.35	174	560
1999-2000	136029	124605	9.15	140	560
2000-2001	172430	188850	10.62	140	560

Sugarcane Development Programme

1. *Lift Irrigation Schemes*

Nothing is more important to a sugar factory than the supply of perennial water to the sugarcane producers. The Parbhani District Co-op. Bank supplied loans to 40 sugarcane growers on the guarantee of the factory for lift irrigation scheme. More and more cane growers are taking the benefit of the scheme.

(b) Purna SSK Ltd., Wasmatnagar, Wasmat

Purna SSK Ltd. was registered in 1970 with production capacity of 1250 TCD. Production capacity of 1250 TCD was expanded in 1990 to 2500 TCD. The factory covers the area of five Talukas that are Parbhani, Wasmatnagar, Hingoli, Jintur and Nanded. The number of villages covered by area of operation is 238. The operational details of the factory are as follows[8]:

Table—3.8: Sugar Production (1991-92 to 2000-01)

Year	*Sugarcane Crushed M.T.*	*Sugar Produced (Quintel)*	*Recovery (%)*	*Gross Working Days*	*Final Price Paid to Growers P.T.*
1991-92	366424	412880	10.92	204	370
1992-93	248754	277590	10.89	129	475
1993-94	314699	327280	10.61	146	700
1994-95	461052	464107	10.09	235	700
1995-96	371104	358046	9.65	197	460
1996-97	229525	259250	10.29	127	510
1997-98	254500	276521	10.41	134	688
1998-99	330011	358791	10.41	166	637
1999-2000	437941	473855	10.78	202	617
2000-2001	320041	353351	10.78	146	712

Development Programmes

The factory had a planned programme in plantation of nursery on their own farm. The sugarcane seeding of different varieties were planted in different specified areas allotted to each variety. This method had ensured matured sugarcane supply throughout the extended season. Sugarcane development programme of the factory had been targeted to achieve a particular objective and that is to raise recovery rate of sugarcane. It is clear from above table that the factory had been more or less successful in achieving the target. The recovery rate was satisfactory. This result was possible as various schemes of development were planned and implemented successfully.

1. Supply of Fertilizer

The factory supplies compost manures and chemical fertilizers to the sugarcane growers. The sugarcane yield and the recovery rate mostly depend on the use of manures and fertilizers.

NANDED DISTRICT

Following two factories were selected for study from Nanded district.

(a) Shankar SSK Ltd., Waghalwada, Tq. Bhokar

(b) Godawari Manar SSK Ltd., Shankernagar, Tq. Biloli

(a) Shankar SSK Ltd.

Shankar SSK Ltd. was registered in 1984 with production capacity of 1250 TCD. At present crushing capacity of the factory is 1250 TCD. The factory covers an area of three Talukas of Nanded district that are Bhokar, Biloli and Nanded. The number of villages covered by area of operation is 184. The operational details of the factory are as follows[9].

Table—3.9: Sugar Production (1991-92 to 2000-01)

Year	*Sugarcane Crushed M.T.*	*Sugar Produced (Quintel)*	*Recovery (%)*	*Gross Working Days*	*Final Price Paid to Growers P.T.*
1991-92	256191	274785	10.65	187	365
1992-93	129470	134151	10.38	119	447
1993-94	146811	148584	10.10	121	646
1994-95	286629	268190	9.35	225	622
1995-96	249196	246500	9.48	212	510
1996-97	155936	157415	10.00	141	510
1997-98	106091	106353	10.03	125	540
1998-99	173501	180261	10.36	141	615
1999-2000	210532	217722	10.33	198	613
2000-2001	146373	147310	10.08	119	620

Development Programmes

The development programme of this factory has been set up to achieve one particular objective and that is to raise the recovery rate of sugarcane. The factory has been more or less successful in achieving the targets. The schemes planned by the factory can briefly be stated as given below:

1. *Supply of Fertilizer*

To improve the sugar recovery rate, proper use of fertilizer is necessary. The factory supplies compost manures and chemical fertilizers to the sugarcane growers. The sugarcane yield and the recovery rate mostly depend on the use of manures and fertilizers. The use of these need careful vigilance and agricultural officers look after them.

(b) Godawari Manar SSK Ltd., Shankar Nagar, Biloli

Godawari Manar SSK Ltd. was registered in 1976 with production capacity of 1250 TCD. At present installed production capacity is 2500 TCD. The factory covers an area of three talukas that are Biloli, Degloor and Mukhed. The number of villages covered by area of operation is 466. The operational details of the factory are as follows[10]:

Table—3.10: Sugar Production (1991-92 to 2000-01)

Year	*Sugarcane Crushed M.T.*	*Sugar Produced (Quintel)*	*Recovery (%)*	*Gross Working Days*	*Final Price Paid to Growers P.T.*
1991-92	282093	308590	10.90	186	357
1992-93	177509	181875	10.45	124	400
1993-94	203827	216145	10.40	122	400
1994-95	453927	426700	9.34	242	561
1995-96	366730	340350	9.03	207	460
1996-97	282718	290100	10.07	135	460
1997-98	99448	84170	9.02	100	540
1998-99	252494	251520	9.85	134	567
1999-00	364271	346740	9.42	189	560
2000-2001	268022	265520	9.81	136	572

LATUR DISTRICT

Following two factories were selected for study from Latur district:

(a) Jai Jawan Jai Kisan SSK Ltd., Nalegaon , Tq. Chakur.

(b) Manjra Shetkari SSK Ltd., Vilasnagar, Latur.

(a) Jai Jawan Jai Kisan SSL Ltd., Nalegaon, Tq. Chakur

Jai Jawan Jai Kisan SSK Ltd., was registered in 1982 with a cane crushing capacity of 1250 TCD. The factory is working in seven talukas of Latur district. They are Ahmadpur, Latur, Nilanga, Udgir, Ausa , Chakur and Renapur. Villages covered under area of operation of this factory are 290. The operational details of the factory are as follows[11]:

Table—3.11: Sugar Production (1991-92 to 2000-01)

Year	Sugarcane Crushed M.T.	Sugar Produced (Quintel)	Recovery (%)	Gross Working Days	Final Price Paid to Growers P.T.
1992-93	149386	153925	10.31	105	426
1993-94	112521	155282	10.24	102	625
1994-95	299453	304240	10.16	221	676
1995-96	273990	279025	10.19	200	580
1996-97	177581	197940	11.16	119	715
1997-98	234877	251040	10.70	149	801
1998-99	231447	264751	11.45	1163	802
1999-2000	310173	365381	11.80	204	805
2000-2001	296147	338265	11.42	169	810

Development Programmes

1. *Supply of Improved Sugarcane Seedling*

The factory had a planned programme in plantation. The seedlings of different varieties were planted in different specified areas allotted to each variety. This method had ensured matured sugarcane supply throughout the crushing season. To achieve the highest rate of recovery, sugarcane seedlings from two research centres viz. V.S.I. Pune and Padegaon, were collected and distributed to farmers. New varieties supplied were Co-86032 and Co-7714.

2. *Competition for Higher Sugarcane Production*

The factory has initiated competitive spirit among the sugarcane growers. Names of the growers who achieve the highest cane yield per acre are circulated among members. Those farmers with the highest yields are given special recognition and award of 10 gms gold medal. This feeling of competition among farmers has helped the factory to achieve higher yield per acre.

(b) Manjra Shetkari SSK Ltd., Vikasnagar, Latur

Manjra Shetkari SSK Ltd. was registered in 1984 with a production capacity of 1250 TCD. Production capacity was expanded in 1997 to 2500 TCD. The factory covers an area of two talukas that are Latur and Ausa. The number of villages covered under area of operation is 145. The operational details of the factory are as follows[12].

Table—3.12: Sugar Production (1991-92 to 2000-01)

Year	*Sugarcane Crushed M.T.*	*Sugar Produced (Quintel)*	*Recovery (%)*	*Gross Working Days*	*Final Price Paid to Growers P.T.*
1991-92	355534	416122	11.80	212	525
1992-93	291140	322335	11.14	142	590
1993-94	304800	355900	11.80	146	876
1994-95	516091	585270	11.45	227	842
1995-96	409705	461595	11.27	189	805
1996-97	283308	324550	11.46	136	815
1997-98	468601	576275	12.30	176	940
1998-99	413313	518380	12.56	169	1011
1999-2000	579196	744830	12.86	212	940
2000-2001	583815	762900	13.07	179	1021

Sugarcane Development Programmes

The development programmes of this factory has been set up to achieve one particular objective that is to raise the recovery rate of the sugarcane. It is seen from the above table (production statistics) that the factory has been successful in achieving the targets. The recovery rate has consistently been above 11 per cent. This achievement can only be possible when various schemes of development are planned and implemented successfully. The schemes planned out can briefly be stated as given below:

1. *Supply of Improved Sugarcane Seedlings*

Sugarcane seedlings from research centre viz. Padegaon, V.S.I. were collected and distributed to farmers. New varieties supplied were Co. M. 7714 and Co. C. 671. Factory provides the amount of Rs. 2500 with low interest rate for the cultivation of improved sugarcane seeds.

2. Competition for higher sugarcane production

The factory has initiated competitive spirit amongst the sugarcane growers. Names of the growers who achieve the highest cane yield per acre are circulated among the members. These farmers with highest yields are given Rs. 5001 for first, Rs. 4001 for second and Rs 3001 for third. This feeling of competition among farmers has helped the factory to achieve higher yield per acre.

OSMANABAD DISTRICT

Following two factories were selected from Osmanabad district:

(a) Tuljabhavani Shetkari SSK Ltd., Tuljapur

(b) Terna SSK Ltd., Ternanagar, Dhoki, Osmanabad.

(a) Tuljabhavani Shetkari SSK Ltd.

Tuljabhavani Shetkari SSK Ltd. was registered in 1983 with crushing capacity of 1250 TCD. The factory is working in Tuljapur taluka of Osmanabad district. The number of villages covered by area of operation of the factory is 108. The operational details are as follows:

Table—3.13: Sugar Production (1991-92 to 2000-01)

Year	*Sugarcane Crushed M.T.*	*Sugar Produced (Quintel)*	*Recovery (%)*	*Gross Working Days*	*Final Price Paid to Growers P.T.*
1	2	3	4	5	6
1991-92	276732	293905	10.59	155	438
1992-93	175632	171265	9.71	121	423
1993-94	62193	61474	9.82	93	910
1994-95	281737	294125	9.60	215	565
1995-96	231526	222215	9.60	183	460

(Contd...)

1	2	3	4	5	6
1996-97	159262	164040	10.14	125	566
1997-98	193856	197063	10.04	137	648
1998-99	202048	221285	10.84	155	617
1999-2000	338288	329535	9.71	213	643
2000-2001	250257	235293	9.40	170	668

Sugarcane Development Programmes

It is observed that the factory has not planned any sugarcane development programme for its own benefit and for the benefit of the farmers till the year 1996-97. But the factory was encouraging the cane cultivators to cultivate the cane Co. 86032 variety which was found good for sugar recovery.

1. Tree Plantation

Near about 1 lakh plants were planted on Karkhana site in 400 acres of land. The plants are Mango, Bor, Naral, Nilgiri and Sagwan. The tree plantation programme was developed under the supervision of Agriculture department of the factory.

2. Compost Fertilizers

Imbalanced use of chemical fertilizers are found unsuitable to the fertility of land. Tuljabhavani SSK Ltd. installed compost manures project to provide manures to the cultivator members of the factory.

(b) Terna SSK Ltd., Ternanagar, Osmanabad

Terna SSK Ltd. was registered in 1965 with a production capacity of 1250 TCD. At present production capacity is 3500 TCD. The factory covers the area of three talukas that are Osmanabad, Kallam and Latur. The number of villages covered by area of operation is 171. The operational details of the factory are as follows[14]:

Table—3.14: Sugar Production (1991-92 to 2000-01)

Year	*Sugarcane Crushed M.T.*	*Sugar Produced (Quintel)*	*Recovery (%)*	*Gross Working Days*	*Final Price Paid to Growers P.T.*
1991-92	407056	426600	10.42	163	321
1992-93	204833	206485	10.03	115	400
1993-94	147287	138785	9.23	98	600
1994-95	604818	639140	10.54	220	918
1995-96	574909	554425	9.63	216	460
1996-97	372481	369555	9.92	126	713
1997-98	565438	629871	11.00	160	802
1998-99	608522	689028	11.32	177	940
1999-2000	870920	1018626	11.70	228	940
2000-2001	743605	881176	11.85	210	1185

1. Sugarcane Development Programmes

The factory developed its own nursery covering 12 acres area and cultivated new varieties which were found useful. The plots for nurseries were allotted to member farmers. The factory has adopted a different plan of supplying manures and fertilizers to the member cultivators. The member who borrows money from co-operative banks for this purpose, the factory stands as a guarantor for the loan.

2. Supply of Improved Sugarcane Seedlings

Sugarcane seedling from research centres viz. Padegaon and V.S.I. Pune were collected and distributed to member farmers for attaining high rate of recovery. New varieties Co. M. 7714, Co. 7219 Co. 850074, etc. were supplied to the cane cultivators. These new varieties of sugarcane were found more suitable for improving the recovery rate.

REFERENCES

1. Annual Reports of Shri Sant Eknath SSK Ltd., Eknathnagar, Paithan, from 1991-92 to 2000-01.
2. Annual Reports of Siddheshwar SSK Ltd., Maniknagar, Sillod, from 1991-92 to 2000-01.

3. Annual Reports of Jalna SSK Ltd., Ramnagar, Jalna, from 1991-92 to 2000-01.
4. Annual Reports of Samarth SSK Ltd., Ankushnagar, Ambad, from 1991-92 to 2000-01.
5. Annual Reports of Gajanan SSK Ltd., Rajuri, Beed, from 1991-92 to 2000-01.
6. Annual Reports of Jai Bhavani SSK Ltd., Shivajinagar, Georai, from 1991-92 to 2000-01.
7. Annual Reports of Godawari Dudhana SSK Ltd., Pathri, from 1991-92 to 2000-01.
8. Annual Reports of Purna SSK Ltd., Wasmatnagar, Wasmat, from 1991-92 to 2000-01.
9. Annual Reports of Shankar SSK Ltd., Wagalwada, Bhokar, from 1991-92 to 2000-01.
10. Annual Reports of Godawari Manar SSK Ltd., Shankarnagar, Biloli, from 1991-92 to 2000-01, Performance of Sugar Industry, Season 1999-2000 and 2000-2001, V.S.I. Manjari, Pune.
11. Annual Reports of Jai Jawan Jai Kisan SSK Ltd., L.B. Shatri, Tq. Chakur, from 1991-92 to 2000-01.
12. Annual Reports of Manjra SSK Ltd., Vilasnagar, Latur, from 1991-92 to 2000-01.
13. Annual Reports of Tuljabhavani SSK Ltd., Tuljapur, from 1991-92 to 2000-01.
14. Annual Reports of Terna SSK Ltd., Ternanagar, Osmanabad, from 1991-92 to 2000-01.

4

Working Capital Management

Trends and Liquidity Analysis

Introduction

Working capital is lifeblood of business enterprises. It has been now established that, the working capital utilisations magnifies the profitability of an enterprise considerably. The firms have therefore, to optimize, the use of limited available sources through efficient and effective management of working capital.

Working capital management is the integral part of financial management, as the utilisation of fixed capital is made through working capital. The efficiency of working capital management has been appreciated by well run enterprises from the point of view of both viability and profitability. If the working capital is not managed properly, the flow of money gets blocked; payment of outstanding expenses is frequently postponed. All this results into stoppage of operations, which leads the enterprises to sickness. Hence it is necessary for enterprises to manage the working capital so as to remain outside of sick zone and earn profits.

The importance of working capital management is emphasised by the fact that the manner of administration of working capital determines, to great extent, success or failure of overall operations of an organisation. Therefore proper management of working capital is crucial importance for the success of an organisation. Hence, it becomes necessary to understand the concept of working capital management.

Concepts of Working Capital

Working capital is that part of capital which is available for using to carry out the routine or regular business operations. For example, the capital required for purchasing of raw materials, carrying out production activity, investment in finished stocks and stores, and payments to the labourers, etc., is regarded as working capital. In brief, it is the capital with which the business is run.

The major components of the current assets are:

Inventories

(i) Raw materials;

(ii) Work in process or progress;

(iii) Finished Goods and others;

Sundry Debtors

Loans and Advances (Short-term)

Cash-in-hand and Cash in Bank balances.

The term current liabilities is used to denote such type of current liabilities which are to be paid during the course of business out of business income. These liabilities mature within a short period of time. The components of current liabilities are:

Sundry creditors;

Short term advances.

Short-term loans: (Commercial banks and others), and Bank overdraft.

Outstanding Expenses

Gross working capital is the total of all the current assets. Net working capital is the difference between the current liabilities and current assets. The management of working capital refers to both, i.e., management of current assets and current liabilities. "The Gross Working Capital" may be used to refer to the total current assets and "Net Working Capital" to refer to the surplus of current assets over current liabilities[1].

Concept of Working Capital Management

Working capital is a continuously changing phenomenon. The reason is that because of business transactions of a particular nature current assets are short-lived investments that are continually being converted into other asset types. For example, cash is used to purchase inventory items, these inventory items eventually become account receivables when they are sold on credit and finally receivables are convened into cash when they are collected. This process is known as current asset conversion cycle[2]. In addition, current assets are affected by current liabilities. The nature of working capital is particular, that it has various components like cash, inventories, receivables, etc. Taken together the current assets and current liabilities for working capital and considering huge number of factors that are influencing working capital management refers to all aspects of the administration of both current assets and current liabilities[3].

Working capital management answers the following questions:

1. How much is the need of working capital?
2. What should be the optimum investment in current assets?
3. What should be the optimum proportion between long-term and short-term sources of funds to finance working capital?
4. Which appropriate source's finance should be used?
5. What should be the relationship between current assets and current liabilities?

To conclude, working capital management is the application of management principles to current assets and current liabilities to maintain liquidity and profitability of the firm through planning and control techniques.

Working Capital in Co-operative Sugar Factories

The information pertaining to working capital management practices followed in the sample co-operative sugar factories are being extracted with the help of discussions with the officers of the factory. Working capital management practices are being examined from different dimensions like concept of working capital, types of working capital, components of working capital, determinants of working capital, adequacy of working capital pattern of working capital management, working capital policy, methods of forecasting working capital, financing of working capital and dealing with surplus and deficit working capital.

Working capital of a co-operative sugar factory is an amount required for the working of the factory. Working of the co-operative sugar factory relates to crushing of sugarcane and producing sugar. As the sugarcane crop is a seasonal perishable commodity, the manufacturing of sugar is made in the harvesting season of sugarcane. Working of a sugar factory can be divided into two parts as working in crushing season in which manufacturing function continues and sugar is produced, and working in non-season in which there is no manufacturing of sugar and functions except production are performed. In both the parts, funds are required for day to day operations is called as working capital. Working capital of co-operative sugar factory is an amount required to purchase sugarcane, gunny bags, consumables store and to meet office and administration expenses and to finance debtors and receivables. In a co-operative sugar factory the amount required as working capital is determined by the time taken by operating cycle. Lesser the time lesser the amount of working capital and vice versa. In co-operative sugar factory, duration of operating cycle is lengthy and time consuming as sugar sales are regulated by release of quota mechanism of Central Government. The new policy on sugar may be useful to the sugar factories. Co-operative sugar factory requires huge amount for working capital as duration of finished goods conversion is time consuming. Large amount is blocked in finished goods inventories, which results into higher interest cost.

Types of Working Capital

As discussed earlier, the production of a sugar factory is seasonal as the raw material sugarcane is seasonally available. The production season, which is particularly known as crushing season, starts in the month of October/November and ends in April/May every year. The period of crushing season is about 5 to 7 months. In exceptional case it may extend to 8 months also as the harvesting season lengthens. The period other than crushing season is called off season or per season. The duration of this period is 5 to 7 months, which starts in the month of April/May and ends in October/November every year. In this period, there is no manufacturing function, as the cane is not available but other functions like office administration and sales are continued.

The requirement of working capital in 'crushing season' and 'off season' are different and thus it can be divided into two types as working capital in crushing season and working capital in off season or pre-season. During off season working capital is required for purchase of stores and spares, repairs and maintenance of plant and machinery, payment of salaries and office expenses, payment of advance to harvesting and transporting labourers and other miscellaneous expenses. During crushing season working capital is required for purchase of sugar cane, payment of harvesting and transportation expenses, salary and wages of factory workers and office workers and other expenses. The amount of working capital required in crushing season is much more than what is required in off season.

The working capital of a co-operative sugar factory may also be termed as 'permanent working capital' and 'temporary working capital'. Some portion of stores and spares and sugar are permanently held in inventories. The amount blocked in these inventories may be termed as permanent working capital and remaining as temporary. Major item of permanent working capital is the sugar in stock. Government regulates sugar sales through Monthly Release mechanism and hence the sales can't be made in excess of the release quota sanctioned by the government. As the rate of sales is lower than the rate of production, stock of sugar is compulsorily held by sugar factories.

Structure of Working Capital

For a manufacturing concern, working capital is needed to finance the current assets such as cash, inventories and receivables as operating cycle requires certain time to recover the cash through transactions. The items of current assets determine the structure of working capital or components of working capital. The concept of gross working capital also implies the components of working capital which are the items of current assets. As per the data collected from co-operative sugar factories surveyed, the components of working capital are:

(i) Cash or bank balances including postal savings.

(ii) Inventories, which includes stock of stores and spares, gunny bags, chemicals, other consumable stores raw sugar and stock of finished sugar.

(iii) Receivables, which include advances to harvesting and transporting contractor, advance to farmer, advances to repairs and maintenance, contractors' and employees' prepaid expenses and occasional deposits.

Marketable securities or short term investments are not found in the co-operative sugar factories studied. Marketable securities are items of current assets and thus components of working capital, generally used to invest short-term surplus cash but it is not used in co-operative sugar factories. The reason is that the surplus cash is used to reduce the short-term loan balances and to reduce the interest cost.

Pattern of Working Capital Management

Working capital management is an important part of financial management which has a direct relation with profit. The responsibility of working capital management should be assigned to a group of experts and experienced employees. In all co-operative sugar factories the pattern of management of working capital is identical.

Managing Director is assisted by Chief Accountant and Staff of accounting department. Accounts department prepares working capital budget for crushing season and off season under the guidance of Managing Director and Board of Directors in consultation with the heads of various departments, like production, stores, sugar sales and cane purchases. Working capital loan proposals are submitted to banks every year and finance is obtained. As per the Government regulations working capital proposals of co-operative sugar factories are assessed by NABARD and recommended to Maharashtra state co-operative bank or D.C.C. bank. These banks finance working capital for period of one year. The loan is to be refunded through sales proceeds of sugar throughout the year. If any balance remains unpaid it is adjusted with next year's working capital loan.

Financing of Working Capital

The working capital finance is the unique feature of co-operative sugar factories. Profit is not the objective of co-operative sugar factories. Any surplus remains after meeting all expenses of production is distributed as cane price among cane supplying farmers. These are no owned source of working capital finance. Every year working capital finance is to be taken from banks. Co-operative sugar factories are joint ventures of State Government and farmers and so working capital finance is provided to factories on the guarantee of State Government Finance proposals are prepared by sugar factories every year for pre-season finance and season finance. These proposals are based on production target. NABARD assesses these proposals and recommends to co-operative banks and banks provide finance to sugar factories. This is a uniform method of financing working capital applicable to co-operative sugar industry in Maharashtra and similarly in Marathwada. While assessing working capital finance proposals of sugar factories, NABARD observes the guidelines of Central Government regarding minimum statutory price of cane purchases and harvesting and transportation cost. Pre-seasonal finance is made on clean cash credit account and seasonal finance is made through pledge and hypothecation of inventories.

Up to April 2000 the working capital limits have sanctioned by D.C.C. banks or M.S.C. bank under the guidance of NABARD under Credit Authorization Scheme (CAS). But from April 2000 onwards CAS is substituted by CMA (Credit Monitoring Arrangements). Hence co-operative sugar factories are not needed to have a recommendation of NABARD. The financing banks are authorized to assess the proposals and make working capital finance at their own (NABARD's letter No. NS/ACD/CAS/H-67/A-75/2000-2001 Circular No. 01 dated 24th April, 2000).

Working Capital Trends

Business is continuing process. It is very difficult to find complete information by way of analysing the financial statements of one year. Therefore it becomes necessary for an analyst to determine direction and tendency of business. The direction and tendency of business can be determined by reviewing the past data relating to the problem under study. Trend analysis helps to judge the tendency of business.

Concept of Trend and Trend Analysis

The review and appraisal of tendency in accounting variables is nothing but trend analysis. The term trend is very commonly used in day-to-day conversation. Trend is also called as secular or long-term trend, is the basic tendency of production, sales, income, current assets or current liabilities etc. to grow or decrease over a given period of time[4]. The trend refers to the series of facts and figures related to various periods. Time series of accounting figures related to particular area shows its behaviour in terms of decrease or increase over a period. The direction of behaviour may be termed as trend.

Now it is generally accepted that to compute trend, the period must cover at least four or five complete accounting cycles. An account cycle generally consists of twelve months period[5].

Working Capital Trends in Co-operative Sugar Factories

Working capital trend analysis indicate the changes which have taken place from time to time in working capital and individual component of working capital like current assets and current liabilities on the basis of any normal base year. To analyse the trend in detail percentage of individual items of current assets, viz. inventories, receivables and cash and bank balances and current liabilities, viz. creditors, payables, etc. may also be calculated. Since the trend ratios indicate the trends of various statement items across the years, they provide horizontal analysis of various items of working capital. It is a dynamic study of the behaviour of the items with the passage of time. For the purpose of forming an opinion as to the satisfaction of the trend of a certain item, it is necessary to compare it with the trend of some related items in the working capital statements.

An attempt has been made to analyse the working capital trends in co-operative sugar factories under study by examining the following aspects of working capital.

(*a*) Current assets trend;

(*b*) Current liabilities trend.

The discussions on these aspects is made on the basis of the statistical data collected through annual reports from the sugar factories selected for study. The analysis is made for the study period for ten years, i.e. from 1991-92 to 2000-01. Factory-wise, year-wise data is used for analysis and inter-year and inter-factory comparison is made.

Current Assets Trend

The objective of examining the current assets trend is to make the analysis of gross working capital. This analysis is made by examining size and growth of gross working capital, indices of working capital, share of components of gross working capital in total gross working capital of co-operative sugar factories under study.

(i) Size and Growth of Gross Working Capital

The size and growth of gross working capital in all fourteen co-operative sugar factories from Marathwada region, for the study period of ten years, i.e. 1991-92 to 2000-01, is shown in Table 4.1. Shri Sant Eknath shows continuous increase in the size of working capital during the entire period from 1991-92 to 2000-01 except 1997-98. In this year there is decrease in the amount of working capital. This is because of decrease in the amount of inventories. In the year 1997-98 it shows decrease in the inventory in i.e. sugar because factory was not in operation. The average working capital per year is Rs. 2300.12. Siddheshwar from the same district shows increase in the working capital for the year 1993-94, 1994-95 and

1996-97. It shows decrease in the amount of working capital for the year 1992-93, 1996-97 and 1997-98. There is considerable decrease in the amount of working capital in the year 1996-97 and 1997-98.

In Jalna district, Jalna shows a continuous growth in the size of working capital except in the year 1996-97 and 1997-98. As factory could not start crushing season in the year 1996-97 and 1997-98 the average amount of working capital was Rs. 2021 lakhs. Samarth having crushing capacity of 2500 TCD from same district, shows increasing trends in the amount of working capital for the last four years of the study period, i.e. 1997-98, 1998-99, 1999-00, 2000-01. In the year 1991-92, 1992-93, 1993-94 there was not very much amount invested in working capital. In 1995-96 and 96-97 it showed increase in size of working capital as compared to the previous year. The average capital was Rs. 4358.20 lakh. Shri Gajanan having crushing capacity of 1250 TCD from Beed district shows decrease in working capital in the year 1992-93 and 1993-94. It shows decrease in the working capital because factory could not starts its crushing season in the year 1992-93 and 1993-94. Thus there was not much stock of sugar in these years. There is slight increase in working capital for the year 1994-95 and 1995-96. Next two years, i.e. 1996-97 and 1997-98, shows decreasing rate in working capital. For the year 1998-99, 1999-00 and 2000-01 it shows considerable increase in the amount of working capital. Jaibhavani having crushing capacity of 2500 TCD from the same district also shows the same type of decreasing trend in the investment of gross working capital in the year 1992-93 and 1994-95. There is continuous increase in the amount of working capital from 1994-95 to 2000-01 except 1998-99. In this year there was decrease in the amount of working capital.

In Parbhani district, Godawari Dudhana shows continuous growth in the size of working capital throughout the period of study except a slight decrease in the year 1993-94 and 1997-98. The average size of working capital is Rs. 2556 lakhs. Purna shows down and upward trend in the size of working capital for the first six years, i.e. 1991-92 to 1996-97. There was increasing trend in the investment of gross working capital for the last four years of the study period, i.e. 1997-98 to 2000-01.

Shankar of Nanded district shows continuous growth in the size of working capital except in the years 1992-93 and 1997-98. The average amount of working capital was Rs. 2592 lakhs per year. Godawari Manar from the same district also shows the same tendency in the growth of working capital. Both the factories show decrease in working capital in the year 1992-93 and 1997-98, because production of sugar was not so high. Thus it affects the stock of inventory. The average size of gross working capital was Rs. 3048 lakhs per year.

In Latur district Jai Jawan Jai Kisan SSK Ltd. shows continuous growth in the size of working capital throughout the period of study, except 1992-93 and 1993-94. The average size of working capital is Rs. 3047 lakhs per year. The Manjara also shows continuous increase in the size of gross working capital throughout the study period except a slight decrease in the year 1998-99. There was considerable decrease in the amount of working capital in the year 1996-97 and 1997-98.

In Osmanabad district Tuljabhavani shows continuous growth in the size of working capital except 1993-94, 1997-98 and 1998-99. The average amount of working capital is Rs. 3076.75 lakhs per year. Terna from the same district shows downward trends in the amount of working capital for first three years of the study period, i.e. 1991-92, 1992-93 and 1993-94. From 1994-95 it shows continuous growth in the size of working capital. Terna shows decrease in first three years because of very low production of sugar. Thereafter it shows continuous growth in crushing and production of sugar. The average amount of working capital was Rs. 8150.86 lakhs per year.

Year-wise comparison of working capital shows that the highest size of working capital is shown by all factories in the last two years of the study period, i.e. 1999-2000 and 2000-01. The highest amount of working capital among all factories is shown by Terna in the year 2000-01 of Rs. 22282.33 lakhs. The lowest size of working capital among all factories shown by Jalna in the year 1997-98 of Rs. 469.57 lakhs and by Gajanan in the same year of Rs. 583.35 lakhs. Inter-factory comparisons show the same pattern of growth of working capital in all factories throughout the period. As per the opinion of experts in the field, an average investment

Table—4.1: Size and Growth of Gross Working Capital in Co-operative Sugar Factories Under Study

Sl.No.	Name of Factories	91-92	92-93	93-94	94-95	95-96	96-97	97-98	98-99	99-00	00-01	Ave
01.	Sant Eknath	1675.58	1729.51	554.22	2022.67	2296.15	2017.51	1192.03	2614.76	3578.81	5319.15	2300
02.	Siddheshwar	1919.92	1509.77	2537.38	3337.07	3920.86	3892.61	1490.05	3712.91	5531.23	6302.87	3415
03.	Jalna	1904.51	1994.08	2378.42	2655.64	2421.98	831.3	469.57	2021.25	2850.1	2682.5	2021
04.	Samrath	1728.71	1920.13	1344.09	3080.93	4778.22	4390.55	3703.9	5831.3	6688.61	10115.95	4358
05.	Gajanan	1077.29	492.97	419.12	1582.96	1339.92	993.92	583.35	2083.6	2856.74	4544.22	1597
06.	Jai Bhavani	2132.24	1761	842.75	3060.85	3100.87	3570.74	3369.75	5291.44	6470.69	6959.98	3656
07.	Godawari Dhudhana	1681.54	2004.65	1515.51	2903.13	3170.26	3286.84	1507.3	2519.61	3021.06	3950.94	2556
08.	Purna	2732.82	3397.05	3042.84	4530.88	4135.81	4255.06	4168.16	4408.81	5337.42	7464.41	4365
09.	Shankar	1611.65	1582.38	1909.57	2363.76	2524.52	2717.93	2300.82	2909	3845.09	4155.23	2592
10.	Godawari Manar	1692.45	1962.28	2512.51	3074.91	3758.38	4568.06	1502.34	3967.51	4806	6272.49	3412
11.	Jai Jawan	1732.07	1616.52	1402.97	2401.79	2515.01	3091.51	3138.15	3600.16	4489.78	6387.03	3047
12.	Manjra	1972.95	2894.2	3019.97	3720.44	4471.72	5474.36	5939.3	5754.4	8989.71	11114.8	5335
13.	Tuljabhavani	1873.68	1957.72	1061.6	2553.58	3081.08	3674.69	3394.74	3347.07	4329.17	5494.19	3077
14.	Terna	3108.53	2585.73	2256.91	5648.45	6902.03	5957.68	8828.15	9013.05	13925.71	22282.33	8151

Source: Annual reports of co-operative sugar factories under study.

of current assets of a co-operative sugar factory of 1250 TCD should be 1500 lakhs to 2000 lakhs per year and factory of 2500 TCD should be 3000 to 4000 lakhs per year. The Table 4.1 shows that this limit is crossed by most of the factories. The reason for the increase in the amount of current assets is nothing but over investment in the inventory of sugar.

Because of record production of sugar from 1994-95 onwards, huge stocks of sugar are held by factories which resulted into growth in the size of current assets, i.e. gross working capital. It has also observed from co-operative sugar factories studied, that the amount of current assets is dominated by only one component, finished goods inventory, i.e. stocks of sugar. The highest and lowest size of current assets, both are the results of the amount invested in finished goods inventory.

(ii) Share of Components of Gross Working Capital in Total Gross Working Capital

The analysis of gross working capital can be made effectively on the basis of the share of its components in total. Table 4.2 gives an idea about the share of each component of gross working capital in total gross working capital. Gross working capital is the total of all current assets which are grouped under three heads, like inventories, receivables and cash and bank balances. Table 4.2 shows year-wise share of inventories, receivables and cash and bank balances in gross working capital of each factory for the study period, i.e. 1991-92 to 2000-01. This analysis throws more light on structure of gross working capital and helps in analyzing working capital problems.

General trend of share of components in sugar factories studied shows that inventories occupies major share in gross working capital in all sugar factories throughout the study period of ten years. The share of inventories ranges from 65% to 87% of gross working capital and share of receivables occupy 11% to 33% share and cash/bank balances occupy only 1% to 6% share in gross working capital. This reveals that increase or decrease in the size of gross working capital is a result of increase or decrease in the size of inventories.

In Aurangabad district, both factories, Sant Eknath and Siddheshwar, show the maximum share of inventories in gross working capital which ranges from 75% to 87% throughout the study period. The share of receivables in gross working capital in both the factories for all years is up to 9% to 23%. The share of cash and bank balances is only 1% to 7% of gross working capital. Only in year 1993-94 Sant Eknath shows a different figures like inventories 27%, receivables 71% and cash and bank balances 2%. But from 1993-94 onwards it also shows the same trend.

In Jalna district, both the factories, Jalna and Samarth show the same pattern of share of components in gross working capital. In this district share of inventories is little less than Aurangabad district, and it ranges 59% to 88%. Share of receivables ranges from 7% to 35% and share of cash and bank ranges from 1% to 7% of gross working capital.

In Beed district, more or less same trend is shown by both factories throughout the study period. In this district share of inventories in gross working capital in both factories over the period of ten years ranges from 60% to 91%. The share of receivables ranges from 10% to 27% and share of cash and bank balance 1% to 5% to gross working capital. Only in the year 1993-94 both factories Gajanan and Jaibhavani show different figures like inventory, receivables and cash.

In Parbhani district, both factories, Godawari Dudhana and Purna, show the same pattern of share component in gross working capital. In this district share of inventories is little less than Beed district, it ranges from 56% to 88%, share of receivables ranges from 19% to 43% and share of cash and bank balance ranges from 1% to 4% of gross working capital. Only in the year 1996-97, it shows different figures like inventory 38%, receivables 62% and cash and bank balances very less amount. But from 1996-97 onwards it also shows the same trend.

In Nanded district, Shankar and Godawari Manar factories show maximum share of inventories in gross working capital, which ranges from 63% to 91%, throughout the study period. The share of receivables in gross working capital in both factories for all years is up to 9% to 23% and share of cash and bank balances is only 0% to 11% of gross working capital. In Parbhani and Nanded districts all the four factories show the same pattern of share of components in gross working capital. Only in 1996-97 Godawari Dudhana shows different figure of inventory because factory could not produce higher stock of sugar. It is found very low production in this year.

In Latur district, Jai Jawan Jai Kisan and Manjra show constant share of components of gross working capital throughout the study period. Much fluctuations are not shown in both factories. Share of inventories in gross working capital ranges from 80% to 92%, receivables ranges from 6% to 16% and share of cash and bank balances ranges from 1% to 5% of gross working capital. In Osmanabad district, Tuljabhavani and Terna, both factories show the same pattern of components in gross working capital. In this district share of inventories is little less than Latur district and it ranges from 66% to 82%. Share of receivables ranges from 16% to 31%, and share of cash and bank balances ranges from 2% to 12% of gross working capital. Only in the year 1993-94 Tuljabhavani shows different figures like inventory 38%, receivables 50% and cash and bank balances 12%. But from 1993-94 onwards it also shows the same trend. In Latur and Osmanabad districts all the four factories show the same pattern of share of components in gross working capital, only in 1993-94 Tuljabhavani shows different figure of inventory because of very low production of sugar in that year.

It can be seen from Table 4.2 that share of components of working capital in all factories over the period of ten years is more or less same irrespective of their profit, loss or location status. It is also found from Table 4.2 that through relative share of component of working capital in per cent rate terms in all sugar factories is more or less same. It is more in absolute terms in 2500 TCD factories and 1250 TCD factories. The amount invested in inventories in 2500 TCD factories like Siddheshwar, Samarth, Jaibhavani, Purna, Godawari Manar, Manjra and Terna are comparatively more than the amount of inventories in 1250 TCD factories, like Sant Eknath, Jalna, Gajanan, Godawari Dudhana, Shankar, Jai Jawan Jai Kisan and Tuljabhavani Shetkari. This is because of high production in the factory of 2500 TCD and low production in factory of 1250 TCD capacity. It can also be seen from Table 4.2 that location does not make any difference in the structure and relative share of components. It shows difference in share in absolute terms.

Table—4.2: Share of Component of Gross Working Capital in Total Working Capital in Co-operative Sugar Factories Under Study

Sl.N.	Name of the Factory	Component	91-92	92-93	93-94	94-95	95-96	96-97	97-98	98-99	99-00	00-01	Average
01.	Sant Eknath	Inventory	82%	78%	27%	81%	82%	75%	58%	80%	76%	81%	72%
		Receivable	17%	20%	71%	18%	17%	23%	41%	19%	16%	15%	26%
		Cash/bank	1%	2%	2%	1%	1%	2%	1%	1%	8%	4%	2%
02.	Siddheshwar	Inventory	81%	79%	86%	83%	84%	84%	52%	81%	83%	87%	80%
		Receivable	13%	14%	9%	15%	14%	15%	46%	17%	14%	11%	17%
		Cash/bank	6%	7%	5%	2%	2%	1%	2%	2%	3%	2%	3%
03.	Jalna	Inventory	81%	87%	85%	84%	88%	59%	31%	79%	79%	88%	76%
		Receivable	13%	10%	12%	16%	10%	35%	57%	18%	17%	12%	20%
		Cash/bank	6%	3%	3%	-	2%	6%	12%	3%	4%	-	4%
04.	Samarth	Inventory	81%	85%	72%	81%	88%	88%	84%	88%	87%	86%	84%
		Receivable	16%	10%	21%	16%	10%	11%	13%	7%	11%	9%	12%
		Cash/bank	3%	5%	7%	3%	2%	1%	3%	5%	2%	5%	4%
05.	Gajanan	Inventory	84%	68%	43%	76%	82%	74%	60%	79%	74%	84%	72%
		Receivable	14%	27%	54%	19%	12%	25%	38%	20%	21%	15%	25%
		Cash/bank	2%	5%	3%	5%	6%	1%	2%	1%	5%	1%	3%
06.	Jai Bhavani	Inventory	86%	70%	42%	91%	88%	82%	73%	81%	82%	87%	78%
		Receivable	12%	13%	53%	6%	10%	17%	22%	17%	15%	12%	18%
		Cash/bank	2%	17%	5%	3%	2%	1%	5%	2%	3%	1%	4%

(Contd...)

1	2	3	4	5	6	7	8	9	10	11	12	13	14
07.	Godawari Dudhana	Inventory	85%	83%	60%	78%	72%	38%	56%	56%	57%	66%	65%
		Receivable	14%	16%	34%	18%	26%	62%	42%	43%	43%	33%	33%
		Cash/bank	1%	1%	6%	4%	2%	–	2%	1%	1%	1%	2%
08.	Purna	Inventory	69%	73%	85%	81%	81%	84%	79%	81%	82%	88%	80%
		Receivable	29%	25%	13%	14%	15%	15%	21%	17%	14%	9%	17%
		Cash/bank	2%	2%	2%	5%	4%	1%	–	2%	4%	3%	3%
09.	Shankar	Inventory	73%	68%	68%	78%	84%	86%	74%	71%	75%	80%	76%
		Receivable	23%	21%	21%	20%	15%	13%	18%	21%	24%	19%	19%
		Cash/bank	4%	11%	11%	2%	1%	1%	8%	8%	1%	1%	5%
10.	Godawari Manar	Inventory	82%	73%	81%	88%	89%	91%	63%	84%	85%	85%	82%
		Receivable	17%	17%	19%	12%	11%	9%	37%	15%	15%	13%	17%
		Cash/bank	1%	10%	–	–	1%	–	–	1%	–	2%	1%
11.	Jai Jawan	Inventory	82%	88%	80%	85%	89%	90%	85%	86%	90%	93%	87%
		Receivable	16%	11%	18%	10%	10%	10%	12%	11%	8%	6%	11%
		Cash/bank	2%	1%	2%	5%	1%	–	3%	3%	2%	1%	2%
12.	Manjra	Inventory	82%	92%	85%	90%	92%	86%	86%	82%	90%	88%	87%
		Receivable	13%	6%	12%	9%	7%	11%	13%	16%	8%	10%	11%
		Cash/bank	5%	2%	3%	1%	1%	3%	1%	2%	2%	2%	2%

(Contd...)

1	2	3	4	5	6	7	8	9	10	11	12	13	14
13.	Tuljabhavani	Inventory	77%	76%	38%	72%	68%	74%	70%	66%	74%	82%	70%
		Receivable	20%	17%	50%	22%	24%	21%	26%	29%	19%	15%	24%
		Cash/bank	3%	7%	12%	6%	8%	5%	4%	5%	7%	3%	6%
14.	Terna SSK	Inventory	82%	70%	67%	74%	70%	76%	68%	75%	75%	66%	72%
		Receivable	16%	21%	26%	24%	22%	22%	25%	21%	21%	31%	23%
		Cash/bank	2%	9%	7%	2%	8%	2%	7%	4%	4%	3%	5%

Source: Annual reports of co-operative sugar factories under study from 1991-92 to 2000-01.

(iii) Working Capital Trend and Indices

Working capital trend can be understood by using trend percentage. To analyse the tendency of working capital in the factories studied, trend indices or trend percentages are used. For calculating indices working capital is taken as total of current assets. Indices are constructed on the base year 1991-92. Table 4.3 shows the gross working capital trend percentage for the study period from 1991-92 to 2000-01.

In Aurangabad district, working capital indices show an increasing trend throughout the study period except 1993-94 and 1997-98. In comparison to 1991-92 the growth indices are increased. In case of Sant Eknath, the index shows decreasing trend in the year 1993-94 and 1997-98 because factory was not in operation. The highest percentage was in the year 2000-01 that of 317%, and 214% in 1999-2000 as compared to 1991-92. The average index is 137. Indices of Siddheshwar show a growth from 78% to 328% during the study period. The average index is 178.

In Jalna district, Jalna shows down and upword trend of working capital indices throughout the study period. It shows fluctuations in working capital on the base year of 1991-92. The highest percentage of index is in the year 1999-2000 that of 150% and 141% in 2000-01. The average index is 106. This is lowest average index among all the factories selected under study. Jalna shows up and down index in the growth of working capital because there were many fluctuations in production of sugar and thus it affects on working capital. Samarth from the same district shows an increasing trend throughout the study period except 1993-94 on the base year 1991-92. It shows highest percentage on the year 2000-01 that of 585%.

In Beed district, the indices shows an increasing trend in Gajanan from 1998-99 onwards. But it shows fluctuations in the indices till 1997-98. The indices of Jaibhavani had been increasing from 1994-95 to 2000-01. The highest index was shown in the year 2000-01. The average index is 171. There are fluctuations in the growth of working capital in Gajanan. The average index in Gajanan is 148. In Nanded district both factories, Shankar and Godawari Manar, shows much fluctuations in the growth of working capital. The indices were increasing in Shankar and Manar from 1992-93 to 1996-97 but again it decreased in 1997-98 and increased in 1998-99.

Table—4.3: Growth Indices of Working Capital in Co.op. Sugar Factories Under Study

Sl.No.	Name of Factory	91-92	92-93	93-94	94-95	95-96	96-97	97-98	98-99	99-00	00-01	Average
01.	Sant Eknath	100	103	33	121	137	120	71	156	214	317	137
02.	Siddheshwar	100	79	132	174	204	202	78	193	288	328	178
03.	Jalna	100	105	125	139	127	44	25	106	150	141	106
04.	Samarth	100	110	78	178	276	254	214	337	387	585	252
05.	Gajanan	100	46	39	147	124	92	54	193	265	422	148
06.	Jai Bhavani	100	82	40	144	145	167	158	248	303	326	171
07.	Godawari Dhudhana	100	119	90	173	189	195	90	150	180	235	152
08.	Purna	100	124	111	166	151	156	153	161	195	273	159
09.	Shankar	100	98	118	147	157	169	143	180	239	258	161
10.	Godawari Manar	100	116	148	182	222	270	89	234	284	371	202
11.	Jai Jawan	100	93	81	139	151	178	181	208	259	369	176
12.	Manjra	100	147	153	189	227	277	301	292	456	563	270
13.	Tuljabhavani	100	104	57	136	164	196	181	179	231	293	164
14.	Terna	100	83	73	182	222	224	284	290	448	717	262

Source: Annual reports of co-operative sugar factories under study from 1991-92 to 2000-01.

In Latur district, Jai Jawan Jai Kisan shows an increasing trend from 1994-95 onwards. The average index is 176. Manjra shows continuous increase in working capital throughout the study period of ten years. In comparison to 1991-92 the growth indices have increased. The highest increase of 563% is recorded by Manjra in 2000-01. As Jai Jawan Jai Kisan shows increase in production of sugar from 1994-95 onwards so there is increase in growth percentage.

In Osmanabad district Tuljabhavani shows increasing trend except in 1992-93 and 1993-94. The average index is 164. Terna shows the same pattern of indices throughout the study period. The growth indices are increased from 1994-95 onwards. The average index is 262. The highest increase of 717% is recorded by Terna in 2000-01.

It can be observed from Table 4.3 that the size of working capital is lowest in all factories in the year 1993-94 and highest in 2000-01. It is also seen from this table that factories having capacity of 2500 TCD, like Siddheshwar, Samarth, Jaibhavani, Purna, Godawari Manar, Manjra and Terna show the higher rate of growth in working capital while factories having capacity of 1250 TCD, like Sant Eknath, Jalna, Gajanan, Godawari Dudhana, Shankar, Jai Jawan Jai Kisan and Tuljabhavani show lower rate of growth in indices. As discussed earlier, this is because of high production results, which increased finished goods inventories and ultimately gross working capital. The lower rate of indices is because of lower production results in low finished goods inventories. The annual average of 1250 TCD factory is comparatively lesser than 2500 TCD factories.

Current Liabilities Trend

The analysis of gross working capital or current assets will be more meaningful when analysis of current liabilities is made together with it. The objective of making such analysis is to analyse the networking concept. The analysis of networking capital is required to examine safety, liquidity and financial strength of business. Current liabilities trend is examined by dealing with size and growth of current liabilities, structure of current liabilities, share of components of current liabilities in total liabilities and current liabilities trend and indices.

(i) Size and Growth of Current Liabilities

Table 4.4 depicts the size and growth of current liabilities in co-operative sugar factories under study. The data of current liabilities is collected and shown in this table for the study period of ten years from 1991-92 to 2000-01 for all fourteen factories. Current liabilities include working capital loans, creditors and outstanding expenses and other short-term payables. This can be seen from Table 4.4, that on an average, the size of current liabilities in all factories in all years is showing increasing trend.

In Aurangabad district, Sant Eknath and Siddheshwar show the increasing trend in current liabilities in all years of the study except 1993-94 and 1997-98. The range of size of current liability in Sant Eknath is from Rs. 1473.96 lakhs in 1993-94 to Rs. 4211.48 lakhs in 2000-01. Both factories show maximum amount of current liabilities in 2000-01. Sant Eknath shows decrease in current liability in the year 1993-94 and 1996-97 because factory could not start its crushing season in these years. The loans taken from banks were at lower level.

In Jalna district Jalna shows increasing trend throughout the study period except in 1996-97 and 1997-98. The reason behind this is that the factory was not in operation in the year 1996-97 and 1997-98. Samarth shows increasing and decreasing trends in the amount of current liability.

In Beed district Gajanan and Jaibhavani show downward and upward trends in the amount of current liability. The minimum amount of current liability, Rs. 1039.11 lakhs, is shown by Gajanan in the year 1992-93 and maximum amount is shown, Rs. 4751.97 lakhs in the year 2000-01. Jaibhavani showed upward and downward trends throughout the study period. It shows minimum amount of current liability, Rs. 2166.58 lakhs, in the year 1993-94 and maximum amount of current liability of Rs. 5619.37 lakhs in the year 2000-01. Both the sugar factories in the district show upward and downward trends in the current liability due to the fluctuations in the production of sugar and thus affecting the working capital loan.

Table—4.4: Size of Current Liabilities in Co-operative Sugar Factories Under Study

Sl.No.	Name of Factory	91-92	92-93	93-94	94-95	95-96	96-97	97-98	98-99	99-00	00-01	Average
01.	Sant Eknath	2295.48	2299.21	1473.96	2955.53	3326.42	3155.33	2312.17	3775.88	3221.62	4211.48	2903
02.	Siddheshwar	745.26	678.95	1107.14	1799.58	1974.8	2143.8	577.1	3148.57	5161.48	5912.29	2325
03.	Jalna	1224.71	1242.52	1278.51	2193.19	2193.2	1249.45	787.26	2127.9	2833.72	3058	1819
04.	Samarth	2816.51	2115.22	1822.68	3520.65	5069.97	4762.07	3579.21	3891.56	3999.87	6766.28	3834
05.	Gajanan	1347.57	1039.11	1066.69	2339.44	2054.13	1703.21	1503.43	2691.13	3841.85	4751.97	2234
06.	Jai Bhavani	2610.22	2587.28	2166.58	3049.52	3134.45	3363.11	2806.97	4101.68	5106.51	5619.37	3455
07.	Godawari Dhudhana	1812.77	2089.32	1638.86	3427.77	4001.66	4279.89	2677.71	3814.35	4375.86	5027.04	3315
08.	Purna	3026.54	3388.15	2863.47	3990.32	3986.89	4342.46	4209.31	4292.58	4844.83	6584.51	4153
09.	Shankar	1363.86	1446.37	2843.8	2415	2568.85	2831.13	2507.33	2915.06	3781.77	4881.74	2755
10.	Godawari Manar	2841.51	3439.83	3994.65	4737.68	5709.7	6036.17	4019.14	5547.06	5181.04	7233.63	4874
11.	Jai Jawan	1568.49	1600.67	1361.96	2275.73	2415.36	2821.5	2872.45	3401.66	4333.49	6660.58	2931
12.	Manjra	1408.09	2255.23	2467.72	3137.16	3890.25	4456.44	4705.69	5114.77	8216.91	9763.86	4542
13.	Tuljabhavani	1424.55	1889.06	1703.92	3288.99	3889.99	4243	3425.12	3482.24	4886.72	5583.05	3382
14.	Terna	2748.42	2642.34	1713.38	5038.94	5476.83	6113	7774.86	8201.67	13361.77	22797.45	7587

Source: Annual reports of co-operative sugar factories under study from 1991-92 to 2000-01.

In Parbhani district, Godawari Dudhana and Purna show increasing trend in the amount of current liabilities throughout the study period, except in 1993-94 and 1997-98. Godawari Dudhana recorded the minimum amount of current liabilities of Rs. 1638.86 lakhs in the year 1993-94 and maximum of Rs. 5027.04 in the year 2000-01. Purna shows minimum Rs. 2863.47 lakhs in the year 1993-94 and maximum Rs. 6584.51 in the year 2000-01. Shankar and Godawari Manar from Nanded district show increasing and decreasing trends in the amount of current liabilities. Minimum amount of current liability of Rs. 1363.86 lakhs is recorded by Shankar in year 1991-92 and maximum of Rs. 4881.74 in the year 2000-01. In Godawari Manar, minimum amount of current liability is recorded Rs. 2841.51 lakhs in year 1991-92 and maximum Rs. 7233.63 lakhs in year 2000-01.

In Latur district, Jai Jawan Jai Kisan and Manjra show an increasing trend in the amount of current liabilities except in year 1993-94. Jai Jawan Jai Kisan recorded a minimum amount of current liability of Rs. 1361.96 lakhs in year 1993-94 and a maximum of Rs. 6660.58 lakhs in the year 2000-01. Manjra showed a continuous increase in liabilities from 1991-92 to 2000-01. The minimum amount of current liability recorded is Rs. 1408.90 lakhs in the year 1991-92 and maximum amount of liability Rs. 9763.86 lakhs in the year 2000-01.

In Osmanabad district, Tuljabhavani shows downward and upward trends in the study period. The minimum amount Rs. 1424.55 lakhs in current liabilities is shown in year 1991-92 and maximum amount of Rs. 5583.05 lakhs shown in the year 2000-01. Terna shows increasing trend in the amount of current liability except in 1992-93 and 1993-94. It is continuously increasing from 1994-95. The minimum amount of current liability is recorded Rs. 1713.38 lakhs in the year 1993-94 and maximum amount of current liability Rs. 22797.45 lakhs is recorded in the year 2000-01.

Current liabilities in co-operative sugar factories include the major item of working capital loan from co-operative banks and payable like creditors and outstanding expenses including interest on various loans. It is obvious that need of working capital increases year after year due to increasing cost of production. Thus amount of working capital loan also increases every year which results in the continuous increase in the size of current liabilities. All factories from each district, show on an average increase in the amount of current liabilities year after year. Table 4.4 reveals that the highest burden of current liabilities was taken by Terna in 2000-01 of Rs. 22797.45 lakhs and Manjra in the year 2000-01 Rs. 9763.86 lakhs. It can also be observed from the table that the burden of current liabilities in the year 1993-94 in all sugar factories studied was lowest and in 2000-01 was highest.

Though current liabilities in all factories studied showed an upward trend, the size of current liabilities of 2500 TCD factories was more than the factories of 1250 TCD capacity. It can be seen from Table 4.3 that the amount of current liabilities in factories like Samarth, Jaibhavani, Purna, Godawari Manar, Manjra and Terna are more throughout the study period than the factories like Sant Eknath, Jalna, Gajanan, Godawari Dudhana, Shankar, Jai Jawan Jai Kisan and Tuljabhawani.

(ii) Share of Components of Current Liabilities in Total Current Liabilities

Table 4.5 shows the share of components of current liabilities in total liabilities. This table gives information about current liabilities as total and share of its components as working capital loans and creditors and outstanding expenses. Every year, a co-operative sugar factory has to take a loan for working capital. This loan is provided by district central co-operative banks or Maharashtra State Co-operative Bank. This working capital loan is an important element of current liabilities. Other components are creditors and outstanding expenses. Table 4.5 gives an idea of working capital loan and creditors and outstanding expenses taken together year-wise for the period of ten years from 1991-92 to 2000-01 for each factory.

In Aurangabad district, Sant Eknath shows an average 35% share of working capital loan and 65% share of creditors and outstanding expenses. Siddheshwar shows the share of working capital loan in current liabilities ranges from 56% to 90% throughout the study period and share of creditors and outstanding expenses ranges 10% to 44% in the study period. In Jalna district,

Table—4.5: Share of Component of Currents Liabilities in Total Current Liabilities in Co-operative Sugar Factories Under Study

Sl.No	Name of Factory	Component	91-92	92-93	93-94	94-95	95-96	96-97	97-98	98-99	99-00	00-01
01.	Sant Eknath	W.C. Loan	19%	25%	37%	22%	31%	27%	38%	53%	64%	69%
		Creditors + OE	81%	75%	63%	78%	69%	73%	62%	47%	36%	31%
02.	Siddheshwar	W.C. Loan	59%	60%	74%	85%	85%	90%	56%	62%	56%	63%
		Creditors + OE	41%	40%	26%	15%	15%	10%	44%	38%	44%	37%
03.	Jalna	W.C. Loan	60%	59%	56%	65%	58%	39%	29%	64%	68%	69%
		Creditors + OE	40%	41%	44%	35%	42%	61%	71%	36%	32%	31%
04.	Samarth	W.C. Loan	46%	59%	33%	43%	54%	54%	58%	70%	66%	79%
		Creditors + OE	54%	41%	67%	57%	46%	46%	42%	30%	34%	21%
05.	Gajanan	W.C. Loan	60%	39%	47%	63%	70%	65%	59%	73%	65%	68%
		Creditors + OE	40%	61%	53%	37%	30%	35%	41%	27%	35%	32%
06.	Jai Bhavani	W.C. Loan	62%	70%	59%	57%	61%	62%	57%	61%	57%	64%
		Creditors + OE	38%	30%	41%	43%	39%	38%	43%	39%	43%	36%
07.	Godawari Dhudhana	W.C. Loan	45%	46%	38%	40%	46%	57%	28%	36%	30%	33%
		Creditors + OE	55%	54%	62%	60%	54%	43%	72%	64%	70%	67%
08.	Purna SSK	W.C. Loan	53%	49%	51%	56%	58%	61%	60%	46%	53%	63%
		Creditors + OE	47%	51%	49%	44%	42%	39%	40%	54%	47%	37%
09.	Shankar SS	W.C. Loan	38%	45%	61%	32%	44%	52%	53%	49%	52%	53%
		Creditors + OE	62%	55%	39%	68%	56%	48%	47%	51%	48%	47%

(Contd...)

1	2	3	4	5	6	7	8	9	10	11	12	13
10.	Godawari Manar	W.C. Loan	34%	36%	39%	53%	54%	54%	34%	60%	60%	66%
		Creditors + OE	66%	64%	61%	47%	46%	46%	66%	40%	40%	34%
11.	Jai Jawan	W.C. Loan	42%	55%	47%	55%	56%	56%	55%	55%	60%	61%
		Creditors + OE	58%	45%	53%	45%	44%	44%	45%	45%	40%	39%
12.	Manjra	W.C. Loan	45%	42%	20%	35%	55%	53%	52%	43%	57%	60%
		Creditors + OE	55%	58%	80%	65%	45%	47%	48%	57%	43%	40%
13.	Tuljabhavani	W.C. Loan	32%	36%	38%	58%	54%	51%	58%	49%	47%	59%
		Creditors + OE	68%	64%	62%	42%	46%	49%	42%	51%	53%	41%
14.	Terna SSK	W.C. Loan	54%	37%	41%	47%	55%	61%	61%	49%	53%	55%
		Creditors + OE	46%	63%	59%	53%	45%	39%	39%	51%	47%	45%

Source: Annual reports of co-operative sugar factories under study from 1991-92 to 2000-01.

Note: 1. W.C. loan = working capital loan.

2. Cr + O E = creditors + outstanding expenses.

working capital loan is little more than creditors and outstanding liabilities. On an average working capital loan in current liabilities is up to 55% and share of creditors and outstanding liabilities is up to 45%. This tendency is shown by Gajanan and Jaibhavani of Beed district. The share of working capital loan in current liabilities ranges from 39% to 73% and share of creditors and outstanding liabilities ranges from 27% to 61% throughout the study period. In Parbhani district Godawari Dudhana having crushing capacity of 1250 TCD shows working capital loan little less than creditors and outstanding expenses. Purna shows the share of working capital loan in current liabilities in the range of 46% to 63% and creditors and outstanding expenses ranges from 37% to 54%. In Nanded district, on an average, both the factories, Shankar and Godawari Manar show the share of working capital loan in current liabilities as near about 50% and creditors and outstanding expenses as 50%.

In Latur district, Jai Jawan Jai Kisan shows the share of working capital loan in current liabilities in the range of 42% to 60% and creditors and outstanding expenses in the range of 40% to 58%. The share of working capital loan in current liabilities of Manjra is in the range of 20% to 60% and creditors and outstanding expenses 40% to 80%. Tuljabhavani of Osmanabad district shows the share of working capital loan in current liabilities in the range of 32% to 59% and creditors and outstanding expenses in the range of 41% to 68%. Terna from the same district show the amount of working capital loan in the range of 37% to 61% and creditors and outstanding expenses in the range of 39% to 63% throughout the study period of ten year.

The highest amount of working capital loan of Rs. 12494.17 lakhs is taken by Terna in 2000-01 and lowest figure is of Siddheshwar of Rs. 577.10 lakhs in the year 1997-98. It can be observed from this table that share of working capital loan in total current liabilities is more in 1250 TCD factories and less in 2500 TCD factories. Share of creditors and outstanding expenses in total current liabilities is more in profit making factories. This means that financially weak factories are supported by banks and financially sound factories are supported by creditors. Location factor does not have its impact over components of current liabilities.

(iii) Current Liabilities Trend and Indices

The trend of current liabilities can be examined well with the help of trend percentages. Table 4.6 shows the current liabilities trend in the co-operative sugar factories studied. Trend indices are the trend percentages based on the year 1991-92. Thus trend percentage of 1991-92 is taken as 100. Trend indices are calculated year-wise for all factories for the period of ten years from 1991-92 to 2000-01. It can be seen from Table 4.6 that on an average trend indices of all factories have been increasing for the whole period except in the year 1993-94.

In Aurangabad district, Sant Eknath shows increasing trend for the period of ten years except 1993-94 and 1997-98. The minimum index is 64% in 1993-94 and maximum is 183% in the year 2000-01. Siddheshwar shows continuous increase in indices for the whole period except 1992-93. The minimum of 77% in the 1998-99 and maximum of 793% in the year 2000-01. In Jalna district, Jalna and Samarth show the same pattern of increase in indices. There is a decrease in indices in the year 1992-93 and 1993-94. Remaining years show increase in indices. The indices show maximum increase 250% in Jalna in the year 2000-01and 240% in Samarth in the same year. In Beed district Gajanan and Jaibhavani show decrease in indices in the year 1992-93, 1993-94 and 1997-98. Remaining years show increase in indices.

In Parbhani district, Godawari Dudhana and Purna show increasing trend throughout the study period except in 1993-94. The maximum increase in indices shown by Godawari Dudhana is 277% in 2000-01 and 218% by Purna in 2000-01. In Nanded district, Shankar and Godawari Manar show increase in indices in all the years of study except in 1997-98. The maximum index in Shankar was in the year 2000-01 and Godawari Manar shows maximum index 212% in the year 1996-97. Jai Jawan Jai Kisan and Manjra from Latur district show continuous increase in indices, except in the year 1993-94 Jai Jawan Jai Kisan was shows a decrease. Maximum index was shown by Jai Jawan Jai Kisan was 424% in the year 2000-01 and maximum by Manjra of 880% in the year 2000-01. Both factories in Osmanabad district show increasing trend indices throughout the study period except in 1992-93 and

Table—4.6: Indices of Current Liabilities in Co-operative Sugar Factories Under Study From 1991-92 to 2000-01

Sl.No.	*Name of Factory*	*91-92*	*92-93*	*93-94*	*94-95*	*95-96*	*96-97*	*97-98*	*98-99*	*99-00*	*00-01*	*Average*
01.	Sant Eknath	100	100	64	129	145	137	101	164	140	183	126
02.	Siddheshwar	100	91	149	241	265	288	77	422	693	793	312
03.	Jalna	100	101	104	179	179	102	64	174	231	250	148
04.	Samarth	100	75	65	125	180	169	127	138	142	240	136
05.	Gajanan	100	77	79	174	152	126	112	200	285	353	166
06.	Jai Bhavani	100	99	83	117	120	129	108	157	196	215	132
07.	Godawari Dhudhana	100	115	90	189	221	236	148	210	241	277	183
08.	Purna	100	112	95	132	132	143	139	142	160	218	123
09.	Shankar	100	106	209	177	188	208	184	214	277	358	202
10.	Godawari Manar	100	121	141	167	201	212	141	195	182	255	172
11.	Jai Jawan	100	102	87	145	154	180	183	217	276	424	187
12.	Manjra	100	203	223	283	351	402	424	461	741	880	407
13.	Tuljabhavani	100	133	120	231	273	298	240	244	343	392	237
14.	Terna	100	96	62	183	199	222	283	298	486	829	276

Source: Annual reports of co-operative sugar factories under study from 1991-92 to 2000-01.

1993-94. Remaining years show an increase in indices. The highest indices recorded was 392% by Tuljabhavani and 829% by Terna in the year 2000-01.

It can be observed from Table 4.6 that all factories, on an average, show the trend of increase. The increase in current liabilities year after year resulted because of increases in the cost and prices of material required for the working of factory. It also gives the annual average growth indices of all sugar factories studied. The average annual growth of current liabilities in the factories studied ranges from 126% to 407%. The growth index is based upon the year 1991-92. It appears from this table that growth index of current liabilities in profit making factories is more and loss making factories have low index of current liabilities.

Efficiency of Working Capital

The efficiency of working capital management in co-operative sugar factories is discussed with the help of working capital turnover ratio.

Working Capital Turnover Ratio

In order to test the efficiency with which networking capital is utilized, many analysis determine the ratio of net sales to networking capital, i.e. turnover of working capital. This is done by dividing the net working capital into net sales indicating whether the business is being operated on a small or large amount of networking capital in relation to sales.

A high working capital turnover may be result of favourable turnover of inventories and receivables or may reflect an inadequacy of networking capital accompanied by low turnovers of inventories and receivables. On the other hand, a low turnover of networking capital may be the outcome of an excess of networking capital, slow turnover of inventories and receivables, a large cash balance or investment. Thus in interpreting the networking capital turnover, the analyst should exercise considerable caution because the working capital turnover ratio is a composite of a number of relationships each one of which should be analysed carefully to account for changes from year to year or between companies[6].

Working capital turnover ratio is an important indicator of efficiency of working capital. It shows the movement of working capital. Working capital turnover ratios of the sugar factories studied, year-wise, for the study period of ten years are shown in Table 4.7. Generally the formula used to compute this ratio is net sale divided by net working capital. But in major co-operative sugar factories studied, there is a negative networking capital, means current liabilities exceed current assets. In such circumstance, the use of this formula is inconvenient, thus formula used to compute this ratio is:

$$\text{Working capital turnover ratio} = \frac{\text{Net sale}}{\text{Gross working capital}}$$

Factory-wise Discussion of Working Capital Turnover Ratio

The interpretation of working capital turnover ratio can be made like higher the ratio—higher the gross working capital turnover—higher the efficiency of working capital; and lower the ratio—lower the turnover—lower the efficiency of working capital. When interpretation is applied to the ratio of the factories studied, it seems that efficiency of working capital management of all factories studied is very poor. This ratio is recommended as sales, 2 times of working capital or current assets. Only two factories showed maximum ratio of 2.31 in the year 1996-97 that is Jalna and 2.24 in 1993-94 that is Sant Eknath due to lower amount of current assets.

In Sant Eknath, the average working capital turnover ratio observed was 0.91, which is significantly lower than the standard of 2 times of sales. It was found that sales of factory registered a fluctuating trend during the study period. The same trend observed was in case of current assets. The lowest working capital turnover ratio was recorded 0.27 in 1994-95, due to considerable lower sales and highest ratio was registered 2.24 in 1993-94, due to little amount of working capital.

Table 4.7 indicates that the average working capital turnover ratio of Siddheshwar was 1.09:1, which is significantly lower than the standard of 2 times of sales. The lowest ratio ascertained was 0.69 in 1993-94, due to lower sales volume. The highest average ratio appeared was 1.77 in 1992-93, which is slightly less than the standard ratio. It indicates good financial position of the factory. Factory showed the ratio more than 1.50 in three years of the study period. It is considerably higher than the industry average.

The average working capital turnover ratio of Jalna was 1.09:1, which is lower than the standard ratio but higher than the industry average. The lowest ratio was recorded 0.70 in 1998-99, due to little sales volume. The highest ratio was recorded 2.31 in 1996-97, which is significantly higher than the standard ratio of 2 times. It indicates healthy financial position of the factory. The factory showed better working capital turnover ratio in first six years of the study period except 1994-95. Thereafter, it is observed that the factory failed to achieve 100% ratio in four years of the study period.

The average working capital turnover ratio of Samarth was observed 0.91, which is equal to the industry average. It was found that net sales of the factory registered a fluctuating trend during the study period. The same trend was observed in case of current assets. The lowest working capital turnover ratio was recorded 0.41 in 1994-95, due to limited sales volume and highest ratio was registered 1.41:1 in 1991-92, due to higher amount of sales.

It is clear that the factory has maintained huge stock of finished goods blocking heavy amount thus higher portion of working capital as compared to sales shows the poor performance of the factory. It may be suggested that factory must try to enhance the sales volume reducing the investment particularly in sugar stock.

The average working capital turnover ratio of Gajanan was 0.89. It was extremely lower than the standard ratio of 2 times. It is also lower than the industry average. It is an indication of feeble financial position. Thus inadequate sales as compared to current assets lead to disappointing ratio. The lowest ratio recorded was 0.27 in 1994-95 denoting the lack of efforts in rising sales, while highest ratio provided 1.80 in 1991-92. Moreover, it is observed that the factory has failed to achieve 100% ratio (1:1) in seven years of the study period, expressing inefficiency of the factory.

Table—4.7: Working Capital Turnover in Co-operative Sugar Factories Under Study

Sr. No.	Name of the factory	91-92	92-93	93-94	94-95	95-96	96-97	97-98	98-99	99-00	00-01	Average
01.	Sant Eknath	1.13	0.92	2.24	0.27	0.67	0.99	0.68	0.68	0.86	0.8	0.92
02.	Siddheshwar	1.58	1.77	0.69	0.85	1.07	0.77	1.83	0.76	0.91	0.75	1.10
03.	Jalna	1.32	1.12	1.17	0.83	1.12	2.31	0.8	0.7	0.81	0.69	1.09
04.	Samarth	1.41	1.12	1.49	0.41	0.7	1.09	0.65	0.86	0.99	0.83	0.96
05.	Gajanan	1.8	1.32	0.39	0.27	1.2	1.11	0.75	0.66	0.68	0.77	0.90
06.	Jai Bhavani	1.27	1.34	1.13	0.27	1.12	0.78	0.65	0.79	0.75	0.89	0.90
07.	Godawari Dhudhana	1.32	0.97	0.9	0.21	0.61	0.59	0.65	0.21	0.38	0.48	0.63
08.	Purna	0.93	0.84	1.21	0.62	1.01	0.91	0.87	0.91	0.69	0.58	0.86
09.	Shankar	1.38	1.34	0.86	0.67	0.93	0.9	0.91	0.72	0.59	0.58	0.89
10.	Godawari Manar	1.37	1.11	0.75	0.82	0.9	0.83	0.87	0.75	0.8	0.69	0.89
11.	Jai Jawan	1.21	1.03	1.21	0.56	1.07	0.87	0.83	0.89	0.84	0.75	0.93
12.	Manjra	1.57	1.01	1.22	1.03	1.15	0.86	0.92	1.34	0.91	0.95	1.10
13.	Tuljabhavani	1.23	0.65	1.69	0.27	0.75	0.62	0.63	0.69	0.83	0.66	0.80
14.	Terna	1.1	1.17	0.82	0.35	0.81	0.84	0.66	0.9	0.77	0.58	0.80
	Industry average	1.33	1.12	1.13	0.53	0.94	0.96	0.84	0.78	0.77	0.71	0.91

Source: Annual reports of co-operative sugar factories under study from 1991-92 to 2000-2001.

The average working capital turnover ratio Jaibhavani observed was 0.90, which is slightly lower than the industry average. It is observed that net sales of the factory registered a fluctuating trend during the study period. The lowest ratio was recorded 0.27 in 1994-95, due to lower sales, and highest ratio registered 1.34 in 1992-93, which was significantly more than the industry average. It showed good financial position of the factory and better efficiency of working capital. It is observed that the ratio is less than 1 six years of the study period, which is considerably below the standard ratio of two times. It indicates the huge amount of inventory against sales.

In Godawari Dudhana, the average working capital turnover ratio observed was 0.63:1. It was extremely lower than the standard ratio of 2 times. It is also lower than the industry average. It is an indication of feeble financial position. The inadequate sales as compared to current assets lead to disappointing ratio. The lowest ratio recorded was 0.21 in 1994-95 and highest ratio recorded was 1.32 in 1991-92. Except in 1991-92 the factory did not achieve 1:1 ratio in any of the years.

The average working capital turnover ratio in Purna was observed 0.86, which is lower than the industry average. The lowest ratio enlisted was 0.58 in 2000-01 expressing high amount of current asset. The highest ratio observed was 1.21 in 1993-94, due to limited stock of inventory. It shows the efficiency of working capital. The factory showed the ratio less than 1 in eight years of the study period. This shows that the factory has maintained huge stock of sugar blocking heavy amount thus higher portion of working capital as compared to sales shows the poor performance of the factory.

In Shankar from Nanded district, the average working capital turnover ratio observed was 0.86:1, which is lower than the industry average. It indicates unsatisfactory sale volume. Lowest ratio was recorded 0.58 in 2000-01. It indicates lower sales as compared to working capital.

The average working capital turnover ratio observed in Godawari Manar was 0.89, which is much closer to the industry average. The highest ratio recorded was 1.32 in 1991-92, due to higher amount of sales, and lowest ratio ascertained was 0.75 in

1993-94 and 1998-99. The factory showed the ratio more than 1 in only two years of the study period. In the rest eight years of the study period the ratio observed was below 1. It indicates the lower sale of sugar as compared to current assets. It is also clear that the factory has maintained huge stock of sugar due to restriction on sale of sugar by the Central Government.

In Jai Jawan Jai Kisan, the average working capital turnover ratio observed was 0.93, which is significantly below the standard of 2 times. However, it is more than the industry average. It show comparatively good position of the factory than Shankar, Purna and Godawari Manar. The factory showed the ratio more than 1 in first three years of the study period. Thereafter, except one year, the ratio observed was less than one throughout the study period.

In Manjra, the average working capital turnover ratio observed was 1.10, which is considerably lower than the standard of 2 times. However, it is significantly more than the industry average. Manjra showed highest average working capital turnover ratio among all sugar factories studied. It indicates satisfactory financial position of the factory in comparison to the remaining factories under study. The lowest ratio appeared was 0.86 in 1996-97, which is slightly less than the industry average. The highest ratio recorded was 1.57 in 1991-92, indicating satisfactory sales volume.

The average working capital turnover ratio of Tuljabhavani was 0.80, which is extremely lower than the standard of 2 times. It is also lower than the industry average. It is an indication of feeble financial position of the factory. The lowest ratio ascertained was 0.27 in 1994-95, due to higher amount of working capital and highest ratio recorded 1.69 in 1993-94, due to higher sales volume. The ratio observed was less than 1 in eight years of the study period. It means factory has failed to achieve 100% ratio (1:1) in eight years of the study period.

In Terna, the average working capital turnover ratio observed was 0.80, which is significantly lower than the industry average. The lowest ratio recorded was 0.35 in 1994-95, due to lower sales volume and highest ratio enlisted was 1.17 in 1992-93. The factory showed the ratio more than 1 in first two years to the study period. Thereafter the ratio observed less than 1 throughout the study period. It is observed that the sales are not increased in proportion to working capital. It affects short-term liquidity position of the factory.

It can be seen from the Table 4.7 that the ratios are minimum in the year 1994-95 in most of the sugar factories studied and maximum in the year 1991-92. The industry average of 1994-95 was 0.53 and that of 1991-92 was 1.33. The lowest ratio recorded by Godawari Dudhana in 1994-95 and 1998-99 was 0.21. It can be seen from the same table that profit making factories have higher ratios and loss making factories have lower ratios. The general trends of working capital turnover ratio seem varied every year. No continuous increase or decrease were shown by any factory. There are ups and downs in the ratios over all the years in all the sugar factories studied.

Table 4.7 also shows the average of ratios out of fourteen factories studied. Three factories show the ratio more than one and remaining eleven factories less than one. Working capital turnover of remaining eleven factories are less than one. Working capital turnover ratio shows the same trend in 1250 TCD and 2500 TCD factories. It shows that the speed of sales in both the factory groups are more or less same.

Fig. 4 (a) effectively shows working capital turnover ratio in co-operative sugar factories studied.

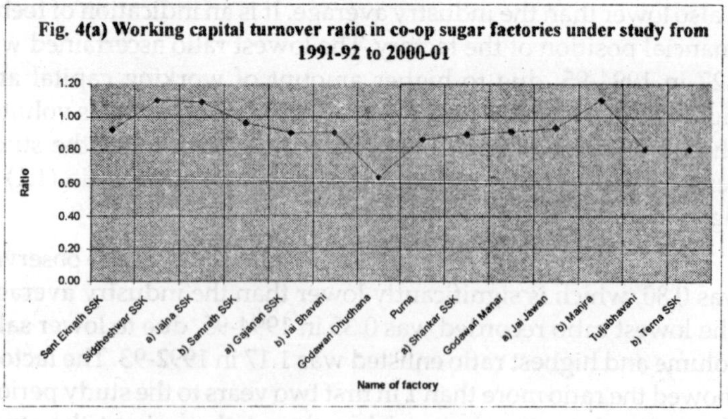

Fig. 4(a) Working capital turnover ratio in co-op sugar factories under study from 1991-92 to 2000-01

Liquidity Analysis

The objective of working capital management is to maintain liquidity of the firm by supplying sufficient funds but keeping the cost of capital under control. Liquidity analysis is a tool to assess the performance of working capital management as to verify how much liquidity is maintained and at what cost. Liquidity analysis enables to judge the efficiency of working capital management. It also provides base to take corrective action to improve the efficiency of working capital. Liquidity analysis together with trend analysis provide the best tool to find out efficiency of working capital management.

Meaning of Liquidity

Liquidity is the ability of an asset to be converted into cash with a significant price concession[7]. The working capital cannot be always held in the form of cash. Therefore it may be in the form of current asset other than cash. While a firm needs cash, the current asset should be quickly convertible to cash. Essential component of liquidity is the time as an asset takes to be converted into cash or time it takes to pay a current liability[8]. More simply, it may be stated as, ability of firm to pay its bills on time. By the term liquidity we mean the debt paying capacity of an undertaking. It refers to the firm's ability to meet the dues of supplier of goods and services and capital[9]. Harry Grass observes that, liquidity of any business results from its ability to generate cash[10]. In short liquidity refers to the capacity of the firm to pay its obligation promptly in time.

Techniques of Liquidity Analysis—Ratio Analysis

A widely used technique of liquidity analysis is ratio analysis. The liquidity is examined by using various ratios:

Concept of Ratio

Ratio is the mathematical relationship between two related items expressed in quantitative form. Ratio is a simple mathematical expression of the relationship of one number to another. Ratio expresses the numerical relationship between two numbers[11]. Ratio is a tool of expression of relationship between two variables. There is simple one number expressed in terms of another. A percentage is simple one number expressed in terms of another. A percentage is one kind of ratio in which base is taken as equaling 100 and the quotient is expressed as 'per hundred' of the base[12].

The techniques of ratio analysis are not limited merely to the computation of ratio but analyse the process of determining and interpreting numerical relationship based on financial statements. The technique is getting wider acceptance in accounting and mathematical world. Helfert has rightly stated: "The ratio analysis provides guides and clues especially in spotting trends towards better or poor performance, and in finding out significant deviation from any average or relatively applicable standard."[13]

Liquidity Analysis in Co-operative Sugar Factories

The following ratios are used for liquidity analysis in co-operative sugar factories under study:

(i) Current ratio

(ii) Quick ratio or acid test ratio

(i) Current Ratio

The current ratio is the traditional ratio used to measure a company's liquidity and is calculated by dividing the total current assets by the total current liabilities. This ratio is designed to assist the decision maker in determining a firm's ability to pay its current liabilities. The higher the ratio, the greater the ability of the company to meet its immediate financial obligations. However, the higher this ratio, the greater the proportion of the company's resources that is tied up in relatively unproductive assets, which have an adverse effect on profitability[14].

Current ratio indicates, in rough fashion, the liquidity of current assets or the ability of business to meet its maturing current obligations. The great popularity of the current ratio reflects the fact that almost everybody, who has occasion to analyse the balance sheet, whether he is primarily interested in short-term or long-term outlook knows that prospects can only be bleak for firms which are not in a position apparently to meet obligations currently becoming due and expected to fall due in the near future. Cash need not be immediately available to meet all current liabilities appearing in the balance sheet but there should be good likelihood of an adequate short-term inflow indicated by the amount of sundry debtors, holding of easily realizable investments and inventories. This constitutes the logic behind the components of current ratio[15].

Current ratios are the most common ratio for measurement of liquidity. Current ratio is the ratio of total current assets to total current liabilities[16]. It is calculated by dividing current assets by current liabilities.

$$\text{Current Ratio} = \frac{\text{Current Assets}}{\text{Current Liabilities}}$$

Current ratio indicates rupees of current assets available for each rupee of current liability. Higher the current ratio, larger the amount available per rupee of current liability. It indicates the high liquidity. A ratio of 2:1 (Two times of current assets to current liabilities) is considered satisfactory as rule of thumb.

If current ratio is less than one, firm could not meet the short-term obligations. For this, let us study the current ratio of sugar factories in Marathwada region.

Table 4.8 reveals the details of current ratio of co-operative sugar factories under study from 1991-92 to 2000-01.

In Sant Eknath the average current ratio of the factory is 0.74:1, which is significantly lower than standard of 2:1. It doesn't express satisfactory position of the factory and factory faces the problem of working capital. The lowest current ratio observed was 0.38 during 1993-94. It indicates the worst short-term liquidity position of the factory and highest current ratio recorded was 1.26 in 2000-01. The analysis of the ratio, during study period reveals that the current ratio is much below the standard. Insufficient current assets as compared to current liabilities have resulted in low ratio.

Table—4.8: Current Ratio in Co-operative Sugar Factories Under Study

Sl.No	*Name of the Factory*	*91-92*	*92-93*	*93-94*	*94-95*	*95-96*	*96-97*	*97-98*	*98-99*	*99-00*	*00-01*	*Average*
01.	Sant Eknath	0.73	0.75	38	0.68	0.69	0.64	0.52	0.69	1.11	1.26	0.74
02.	Siddheshwar	2.58	2.22	2.29	1.85	1.99	1.82	2.58	1.18	1.07	1.07	1.86
03.	Jalna	1.55	1.6	1.86	1.21	1.1	0.67	0.6	0.95	1	0.88	1.14
04.	Samarth	0.61	0.9	0.74	0.88	0.95	0.92	1.03	1.5	1.67	1.49	1.16
05.	Gajanan	0.8	0.47	0.39	0.68	0.65	0.58	0.39	0.77	0.74	0.96	0.64
06.	Jai Bhavani	0.82	0.68	0.39	1	0.99	1.06	1.2	1.29	1.27	1.24	0.99
07.	Godawari Dudhana	1.25	0.96	0.92	0.85	0.79	0.77	0.56	0.66	0.69	0.79	0.82
08.	Purna	0.9	1	1.06	1.14	1.04	0.98	0.99	1.03	1.1	1.13	1.04
09.	Shankar	1.18	1.09	0.67	0.98	0.98	0.96	0.92	1	1.02	0.085	0.96
10.	Godawari Manar	0.6	0.57	0.63	0.65	0.66	0.76	0.4	0.72	0.93	0.87	0.66
11.	Jai Jawan	1.1	1.01	1.03	1.06	1.08	1.1	1.09	1.06	1.04	0.96	1.05
12.	Manjra	1.78	1.28	1.22	1.19	1.15	1.23	1.26	1.12	1.09	1.14	1.25
13.	Tuljabhavani	1.32	1.04	0.62	0.78	0.79	0.87	0.99	0.96	0.89	0.98	0.92
14.	Terna	1.13	0.98	1.32	1.12	1.19	0.97	1.14	1.1	1.04	0.98	1.1
	Industry Average	1.16	1.04	0.96	1.01	1	0.95	0.98	1	1.05	1.04	1.02

Source: Annual reports of co-operative sugar factories under study from 1991-92 to 2000-2001.

The average current ratio of Siddheshwar is 1.86, which is slightly lower than standard ratio. The current ratio of the factory was in the range of 1.07 in 1999-2000 and 2000-2001 and 2.58 in 1991-92 and 1997-1998, which indicates healthy short-term financial position.

The current ratio was less than one in 1998-99 and 2000-2001, expressing financially weak position and inability to meet short-term obligations.

The average current ratio of Jalna is 1.14:1, which is staggering behind the standard ratio 2:1, expressing unsound financial position of the factory. The lowest ratio enlisted was 0.60 in 1997-98 because of limited current assets against current liabilities and highest ratio was 1.86 in 1993-94. Moreover, it is observed that the factory did not achieve 100% ratio in four financial years of the study period.

In Samarth, the average current ratio is observed 1.16:1, which is considerably lower than standard ratio of 2:1. It indicates the poor performance of the factory management. The lowest current ratio observed was 0.61 in 1991-92. It indicates inadequate current assets. It results in inability of the factory in meeting the short-term obligations. Highest current ratio recorded was 1.67 in 1999-2000. The analysis of the ratio shows that the current ratio is much below the standard. It is observed that the current ratio showing increasing trends from 1997-98. It indicates the factory has succeeded in equalizing the current asset with current liabilities in last four years of the study period. The factory has made efforts for good crushing. It resulted in improvement in current ratio.

The average current ratio of Gajanan observed was 0.64. It is considerably lower than standard ratio of 2:1, stating inadequate current asset. It means factory is not able to equalize the current asset and current liabilities. It becomes difficult to meet short-term obligations. The lowest current ratio observed was 0.39 during 1993-94. It shows weak short-term liquidity position of the factory. The highest current ratio recorded was 0.96 in 2000-01. The factory did not achieve even half of the standard ratio of 2:1 even in single year. It reveals that the current ratio is much below the standard.

Insufficient current asset as compared to current liabilities has resulted in low ratio.

In Jaibhavani, average current ratio observed is 0.96:1, which is significantly lower than standard ratio of 2:1. It expresses unsatisfactory performance of current asset and feeble financial position of the factory. The small amount of current asset to current liabilities creates severe crunch in short-term liquidity. However, factory showed improvement in current ratio since 1996-97.

The average current ratio of Godawari Dudhana observed is 0.82:1, which is staggering behind the standard ratio 2:1, expressing weak financial position of the factory. It indicates unsatisfactory performance of the factory. The lowest ratio enlisted was 0.56 in 1997-98 because of limited current asset against current liabilities. The highest ratio recorded was 1.25 in 1991-92. Moreover, it is observed that the factory did not achieve even half of the standard ratio of 2:1 during the study period except in 1991-92. It reveals that the current ratio is much below the standard ratio. It indicates the poor performance of the factory management.

The average current ratio of Purna was 1.04:1, which was lower than the standard ratio. The current ratio of the factory was in the range of 0.90 in 1991-92 and 1.14 in 1994-95. The lowest ratio ascertained was 0.90 in 1991-92 due to limited current asset. The current ratio was observed less than one in three years of the study period. It indicates the weak financial position of the factory. It may be observed that the factory has failed in equalizing the current asset with current liabilities. Hence, its short-term financial position seems to be unsatisfactory. It indicates that liquidity of the factory is determined perpetually.

The average current ratio of Shankar is observed 0.96:1, which is significantly lower than standard ratio of 2:1, expressing unsound financial position of the factory. The lowest ratio enlisted was 0.67:1 in 1993-94. It shows limited current asset against current liabilities. The highest current ratio recorded was 1.18 in 1991-92. The current ratio was observed less than one in seven years of the study period. It indicates the poor financial position of the factory. Hence, its short-term liquidity position seems to be unsatisfactory.

In Godawari Manar, the average current ratio observed is 0.65:1, which is significantly lower than standard ratio of 2:1. The lowest ratio ascertained was 0.40 in 1997-98 and highest in 1999-2000. During the entire period, the ratio was observed below 1, which indicates feeble financial position of the factory. It may be observed that the factory has failed in equalizing the current asset with current liabilities due to low production of sugar during the study period. Current asset includes inventory, i.e. stock of sugar. Thus it affects the current asset.

The average current ratio of Jai Jawan Jai Kisan observed is 1.05:1, which is lower than the standard ratio of 2:1. However, it is slightly more than the industry average of 1.02. There were not much fluctuations in the current ratio during the study period. It was in the range of 0.96 in 2000-01 to 1.10 in 1991-92 and 1996-97. The analysis of the ratio, for the study period, reveals that the current ratio is much below the standard ratio.

The average current ratio of Manjra is 1.25:1, which is also lower than the standard ratio of 2:1. However, it is considerably higher than the industry average of 1.02. The highest ratio enlisted was 1.73 in 1991-92, which indicates strong short-term financial position. The lowest current ratio observed was 1.09 in 1999-2000, which expresses financially weak position of the factory. The factory tried to maintain the ratio above 1.00 during the study period. It is observed that the factory is making efforts for good crushing of sugarcane so as to increase the production and ultimately the current asset.

In Tuljabhavani, the average current ratio observed is 0.92:1, which is considerably lower than the standard ratio of 2:1 and also lower than the industry average. The lowest ratio recorded was 0.62 in 1993-94. In this year industry average was also lower. The highest ratio ascertained was 1.32 in 1991-92. The factory achieved the ratio of more than 1.00 in two years of the study period only. It indicates the weak financial position of the factory. Hence, its short-term liquidity position seems to be unsatisfactory.

The average current ratio of Terna is 1.10:1, which is slightly higher than industry average. However, the ratio is not satisfactory as per financial norms. The lowest ratio appeared was 0.97 in

1996-97 and highest 1.32 in 1993-94. The current ratio was observed below 1.00 in three years of the study period. It showed below1.19 in rest of the years of study period. It indicates that the factory is not able to equalize the current asset and current liabilities.

The current ratio recommended is 2:1, but only Siddheshwar from Aurangabad district has shown current ratio more than 2 in the year 1991-92 to 1993-94 and 1997-98. No other factory has shown this figure during the study period. It can be seen from the Table 4.8 that highest average current ratio of 1.86:1 is shown by Siddheshwar and lowest average current ratio of 0.39 is shown by Gajanan. It is observed that the liquidity position of Siddheshwar is better among all factories studied and poor in the case of Gajanan.

It may be observed from the Table 4.8 that the highest average current ratio is 1.16:1 in 1991-92 and lowest 0.95 in 1996-97.

Fig. 4 (b) effectively shows the current ratio in co-operative sugar factories studied from 1991-92 to 2000-01.

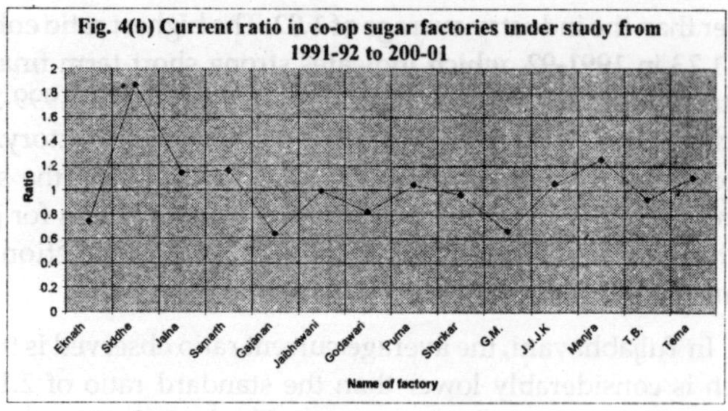

(ii) Quick Ratio or Acid Test Ratio

A supplementary test of the ability of business to meet its current obligations is the quick or acid test ratio. The quick ratio is calculated by dividing the total current assets less inventories by the total current liabilities less bank overdraft. The reason for deducting inventories are regarded as the best liquid of all current assets, and so, this will prove the most difficult to realize at short notice, also it is unusual for a bank overdraft to be withdrawn at short notice, consequently these items are excluded from the computation of quick ratio[17].

Liquidity analysis made through current ratio is supplemented by quick ratio because of the drawbacks of current ratio. Quick ratio is another widely used tool for judging short-term liquidity. The ratio is designed to show the amount of cash available for meeting immediate payments. For calculating this ratio, the total of quick assets is divided by the total of current liabilities. The term quick assets include cash, bank and receivables and easily marketable securities. Inventories are excluded since they take much time to realize, than other current assets. Quick ratio is calculated by following formula.

$$\text{Quick Ratio} = \frac{\text{Quick Assets}}{\text{Current Liabilities}}$$

Acid test ratio of 1:1 or greater is recommended. This ratio is true test of going concern solvency of business.

It is a rigorous and stringent test of a firm to meet current obligations. The rule of thumb is 1:1 for the acid test ratio. If a business has a quick ratio of at least 100%, it is considered to be in a fairly good current financial position[18]. It means, in any circumstance quick assets should not be less than quick liabilities. The ratio is designed to show the amount of cash available for meeting immediate payments.

Factory-wise Quick Ratio

Quick ratio is an index of quick liquidity of the business. Table 4.9 shows quick ratio of fourteen co-operative sugar factories selected for study. Quick ratio is provided for every year for the period of ten years from 1991-92 to 2000-01. Quick ratio is computed by current assets, excluding inventories, by current liabilities.

In Aurangabad district, in Sant Eknath the average acid test ratio for the period of 1991-92 to 2000-01 was 0.18. It was considerably lower than the standard ratio. Lowest liquid ratio observed was 0.12 in 1995-96 and highest 0.26 in 1999-2000, creating a challenge before the factory. It may be observed that the factory has failed in equalising the liquid asset with liquid liabilities. Hence its short-term financial position seems to be unsatisfactory.

The average quick ratio of Siddheshwar for the given period is 0.39:1. It is considerably lower than standard ratio of 1:1, stating inadequate liquid assets. The lowest ratio ascertained was 0.14 in 2000-01, expressing unsatisfactory performance of the factory, and highest ratio enlisted was 1.24 in 1997-98. The factory achieved the standard quick ratio in this year.

In Jalna district, the average quick ratio of Jalna is 0.26 which is also lower than standard ratio of 1:1, denoting that the factory is not able to equalise the liquid assets and current liabilities. It becomes difficult to meet short-term obligations, creating obstacles in continuing the day to day operations. Lowest ratio observed was 0.11 in 2000-01, due to limited quick-assets as against current liabilities, and highest ratio recorded was 0.50 in 1996-97. During the entire period, the ratio was observed below 50%, which indicates feeble financial position of the factory.

The average quick ratio of Samarth is 0.16, which is significantly lower than the standard of 1:1, stating inadequate liquid assets. It results in inability of the factory in meeting the short-term obligations. It creates obstacles in the development process of the factory. The lowest ratio observed was 0.11 in 1991-92, expressing unsatisfactory performance of the factory, and highest ratio enlisted was 0.22 in 1990-2000. The factory did not achieve even half of the standard ratio of 100% even in single year.

In Beed district, the average quick ratio of Gajanan is 0.17 which is significantly lower than the standard ratio of 1:1, denoting that the factory is not able to equalise the liquid assets and current liabilities. It becomes difficult to meet short-term obligations, creating hinderances in continuing the day to day operations. Lowest ratio observed was 0.11 in 1995-96, due to limited quick assets, and highest ratio recorded was 0.22 in 1993-94.

Average quick ratio of Jaibhavani is 0.18: 1. It is considerably lower than the standard of 1:1, stating inadequate liquid assets. The lowest ratio ascertained was 0.09 in 1993-94, expressing very

Table—4.9: Quick Ratio in Co-operative Sugar Factories Under Study

Sl.No.	Name of the Factory	91-92	92-93	93-94	94-95	95-96	96-97	97-98	98-99	99-00	00-01	Average
01.	Sant Eknath	0.13	0.17	0.17	0.13	0.12	0.16	0.21	0.14	0.26	0.24	0.18
02.	Siddheshwar	0.49	0.46	0.32	0.32	0.3	0.29	1.24	0.22	0.18	0.14	0.39
03.	Jalna	0.28	0.21	0.27	0.21	0.27	0.5	0.41	0.2	0.2	0.11	0.26
04.	Samarth	0.11	0.13	0.2	0.17	0.12	0.11	0.16	0.18	0.22	0.2	0.16
05.	Gajanan	0.12	0.15	0.22	0.16	0.11	0.15	0.16	0.16	0.19	0.15	0.17
06.	Jai Bhavani	0.12	0.2	0.23	0.09	0.11	0.2	0.26	0.22	0.22	0.16	0.18
07.	Godawari Dudhana	0.19	0.017	0.37	0.19	0.22	0.47	0.25	0.29	0.29	0.06	0.25
08.	Purna	0.28	0.27	0.16	0.21	0.19	0.15	0.2	0.19	0.21	0.14	0.2
09.	Shankar	0.31	0.35	0.21	0.22	0.16	0.14	0.24	0.29	0.25	0.16	0.23
10.	Godawari Manar	0.1	0.15	0.12	0.07	0.07	0.06	0.15	0.11	0.14	0.13	0.11
11.	Jai Jawan	0.2	0.12	0.21	0.16	0.12	0.11	0.16	0.15	0.11	0.06	0.14
12.	Manjra	0.32	0.11	0.18	0.12	0.1	0.17	0.18	0.2	0.1	0.14	0.16
13.	Tuljabhavani	0.3	0.25	0.39	0.21	0.25	0.22	0.3	0.32	0.23	0.17	0.26
14.	Terna	0.21	0.3	0.42	0.29	0.36	0.27	0.37	0.27	0.26	0.33	0.31
	Industry Average	0.22	0.22	0.25	0.18	0.18	0.21	0.31	0.21	0.2	0.16	0.21

Source: Annual reports of co-operative sugar factories under study from 1991-92 to 2000-2001.

weak performance of the factory, and the highest ratio enlisted was 0.02 in 1997-98. The factory did not achieve even half of the standard ratio of 100% even in single year.

In Parbhani district, the average quick ratio of Godawari Dudhana is 0.25, which is considerably lower than the standard of 1:1. Lowest liquid ratio observed was 0.06 in 2000-01, expressing unsatisfactory performance of the factory, and the highest ratio enlisted was 0.47 in 1996-97. The factory did not achieve even half of the standard ratio of 100% even in single year. It may be observed that the factory has failed in equalising the liquid assets with liquid liabilities. Hence, its short-term financial position seems to be unsatisfactory.

The quick ratio of Purna is 0.20 considerably lower than the standard ratio. Lowest liquid ratio observed was 0.14 in 2000-01 and highest 0.28 in 1991-92, creating a challenge before the factory. It means, the factory has failed in equalising the liquid assets with liabilities.

In Nanded district, the average liquid ratio of Shankar is 0.23:1. It is considerably lower than the standard of 1:1 stating inadequate liquid assets. It results in inability of the factory in meeting the short-term obligations. It creates obstacles in the development process of the factory. The lowest ratio ascertained was 0.14 in 1996-97, expressing unsatisfactory performance of the factory and highest ratio recorded was 0.35 in 1992-93. The factory did not achieve even half of the standard ratio of 100% even in single year.

The average quick ratio of Godawari Manar is 0.11:1, which is significantly lower than the standard of 1:1, denoting that factory is not able to equalise the liquid assets and current liabilities. It becomes difficult to meet the financial obligations, creating hinderance in the day-to-day operations. Lowest ratio observed was 0.06 in 1996-97, due to limited quick assets against current liabilities, and highest ratio recorded was 0.15 in 1992-93. During the entire period, the ratio was observed below 0.15, which indicates feeble financial position of the factory.

In Latur district, the average acid test ratio of Jai Jawan Jai Kisan is 0.14:1, which is considerably lower than the standard of

1:1, stating inadequate liquid assets. Lowest ratio observed was 0.06 in 2000-01, due to limited quick assets as against current liabilities, and highest ratio recorded was 0.20 in 1991-92. During the entire period, the ratio observed was below 20%, which shows weak financial position of the factory. The small amount of quick assets than current liabilities creates severe problems in short-term liquidity.

The average acid test ratio of Manjra is 0.16:1, which is also considerably lower than the standard of 1:1, stating inadequate liquid assets. It results in inability of the factory in meeting the short-term obligations. It creates obstacles in the development process of the factory. The lowest ratio ascertained was 0.10 in 1999-2000, expressing unsatisfactory performance of the factory, and highest ratio enlisted was 0.32 in 1991-92. The factory did not achieve even half of the standard ratio of 100% even in single year. It indicates the weak liquidity position of the factory.

In Osmanabad district, the average liquid ratio of Tulja-bhavani is 0.26:1, which is lower than the standard of 1:1, denoting that factory is not able to equalise the liquid assets and current liabilities. It may have difficulties to meet the financial obligations of the factory. Lowest ratio observed was 0.39 in 1993-94.

The average quick ratio of Terna is 0.31:1, which is significantly lower than standard. The lowest ratio found was 0.21 in 1991-92, expressing unsatisfactory performance of the factory, and highest ratio enlisted was 0.37 in 1997-98. The factory could not achieve even half of the standard ratio of 100% even in single year. It indicates that the liquidity of the factory was very poor.

It can be seen from the table 4.9 that the highest average quick ratio shown in 0.39:1 by Siddheshwar and lowest 0.11:1 by Godawari Manar. It is observed that not a single factory touched the recommended quick ratio 1:1 during the study period. Therefore, it may be recommended that sugar factories should concentrate on strengthening the liquid assets position.

Fig 4. (c) effectively shows quick ratio in co-operative sugar factories studied from 1991-92 to 2000-01.

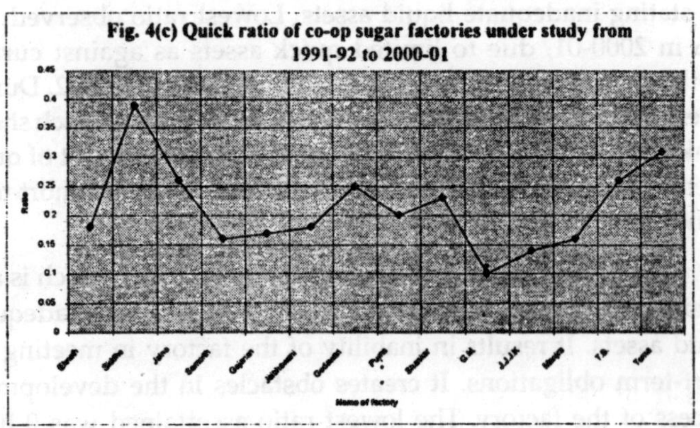

Fig. 4(c) Quick ratio of co-op sugar factories under study from 1991-92 to 2000-01

The quick ratio recommended is 1:1, but not a single factory touched this ratio. It shows very poor liquidity position of the factories studied.

REFERENCES

1. Kuchhal S.C., —Corporate Finance-Principles and Problems, Chaitannya Publishing House, Allahabad, 2nd Edition, 1958, p. 311.

2. Ramesh K.S. Rao. —Financial Management, Macmillan Publishing Co., New York, 1987, p. 517.

3. Weston and Brigham. Essentials of Managerial Finance, The Dryden Press, Japan. 1985, p. 169.

4. Ravi K. Jain, —Working Capital Management of State Enterprises in India, National Publishing House, Jaipur, 1988, p. 83

5. Ravi K. Jain. Op. cit. p. 83.

6. Man Mohan Goyal —Principles of Management Accounting, Sahitya Bhavan, Agra, 1990, p. 457.

7. Vanhorne Wachowiez Tr. —Fundamentals of Financial Management, Prentice Hall of India Pvt. Ltd., New Delhi. 1999, p. 128.

8. V.K. Bhalla, —Working Capital Management—Text and Cases, Anmol Publishing Pvt. Ltd., New Delhi, 1998, p. 185.

9. K.V. Rao, —Management of Working Capital in Public Enterprises, Deep and Deep Publications, New Delhi, 1990, p. 269.

10. Harry Grass - as quoted by Ravi K. Jain, —Working Capital Management of State Enterprises in India, National Publishing House, New Delhi, 1988, p. 83.

11. A.B. Choudhary, —Analysis and Interpretation of Financial Statements Through Financial Ratios, Orient Longmans, Calcutta, 1970, p. 6.

12. Antony and Reece, Management Accounting—Text and Cases, D.B. Tarporwala and Co. Pvt. Ltd., Bombay, 1975, p. 350.

13. Helfert, Erich A., —Techniques of Financial Analysis, —as quoted in "Financial Statements," N.P. Agrawal, p. 10.

14. V.K. Bhalla, op. cit. p. 187.

15. Man Mohan Goyal, op. cit. p. 425.

16. Sharma and Gupta —Management Accounting— S. J. Publishers, Meerut, 1986, p. 232.

17. V.K. Bhalla, op. cit, p. 188.

18. Sharma N.K., —Financial Management and Appraisal, Arihant Publishing House, Jaipur, 1994, p. 110.

5

Inventory Management

Introduction

Inventory occupies very important position in the structure of working capital as it contributes the major part of current assets. Maintaining inventories is necessary to every business because without inventories the operating cycle of the firm cannot continue. Inventories have their impact over the whole activities of the firm as raw material inventory is necessary for continuous production and finished goods inventory is necessary for continued sales. Inventories have their own costs and benefits, so proper management of inventories affect the profitability of the firm.

The term inventory is used for varied meanings. A dictionary meaning of word is 'stock of goods'. The classified definition of inventory is that it is idle resource of any kind having an economic value[1]. From this we can identify inventory as those materials which are procured, stored and used for day to day functioning of the organisation. Inventory is also defined as the goods held for eventual resale by the firm[2]. To the financial it executive, it connotes the value of raw material, consumables, spares, work in progress and finished goods in which company's working capital funds have been invested[3].

It is obvious that if a term inventory applied to a non-manufacturing concern, it includes goods owned by business for sale and when it is used to a manufacturing concern it includes stock of raw material, stores and spares, work in progress and finished goods. In this study the definition of inventory is held related to a manufacturing concern.

Need to Hold Inventories

The classical definition describes the inventory as an idle resource and this definition comes true when inventories are not controlled and managed efficiently. A firm is always keen and careful about the management of this idle resource but still hold huge quantity of inventories for various reasons. When a firm accepts that if inventory is idle, it becomes costly, as carrying and storage costs and investment in inventory goes increasing, the questions arises as to why to invest in inventory.

Economists have established three motives for holding inventories[4].

Transaction motive, precautionary motive and speculative motive.

(i) The transaction motive emphasises the need to maintain inventories to facilitate smooth production and sales operations.

(ii) The precautionary motive necessitates holding of inventories to guard against the risk of unpredictable changes in demand and supply forces and other factors.

(iii) The speculative motive influences the decision to increase or reduce inventories to take advantage of price fluctuations[5].

Stock of finished goods has to be held because production and sales are not instantaneous. A firm cannot produce immediately when goods are demanded by customers. Therefore, to supply finished goods, on regular basis, their stock has to be maintained.[6]

Functions of Inventory Management

To achieve the overall objective of management and to achieve the objective of inventory management, it has to design its function in such a way as to assist its objective attainments. Some important functions of inventory management are discussed below.

(i) Forecasting Inventories

Forecasting inventory need not be emphasised. The systematic marshalling of facts and judgment is essential for sound decision making, planning and control. The most important aspect of this process is the estimation of quantum and value of the future inventory of raw materials and semi-finished goods[7]. Forecasting of inventories is essential for planning, management and control of the inventory. Forecasting of inventories implies quantitative as well as monetary value estimation of inventories.

(ii) Determination of Optimum Level of Inventory

Inadequate and excess inventory situations are costly and harmful to any business enterprise. The prime function of inventory management is to determine the optimum level of inventory and its components. But determination of optimum quantity of inventory is not an easy task. The real problem is to determine the inventory level of which money invested in inventory produces a higher rate of return through these benefits than it would were it invested in some other phase of the business[8].

(iii) Maintaining Adequacy Inventories

If very low inventories are maintained, the company has to encounter frequent stock outs and incur heavy ordering costs. Very large inventories subject the company to heavy inventory carrying costs in addition to an unnecessary tie up of funds. An efficient inventory management, therefore, requires the company to maintain inventories at an optimum level where inventories cost are the minimum and at the same time where there is no stock outs which may result in loss of sale or interruption in the production process[9]. So adequate inventory should be carried by a firm to perform its entire business operations smoothly.

(iv) Control Over Inventories

The fundamental function of inventory management is to keep inventories at an optimum level to get maximum possible return on the funds invested in it. To achieve this, various efforts are made. The entire range of efforts made to achieve this objective may be termed as inventory control techniques. Inventory control is a core part of inventory management and thus the term inventory management and inventory control are used for the same meaning.

Inventory control is a broad term. It refers to the control of raw materials, stores and spares, work-in-progress and finished goods. The concept of inventory control should be understood carefully.

Nature and Components of Inventory in Co-op. Sugar Factories

An inventory occupies a key position in the structure of working capital. To repeat, given the production technique maximisation of income and profit mainly depends on the turnover of working capital. The turnover of the working capital is mostly determined by the turnover of inventories. It is, therefore, quite natural that inventory which helps to maximize profits, occupies the most significant place in the current assets[10].

Inventory represents major current assets investment by most manufacturing firms. Inventory is necessary for "Production sale process" of the firm to operate with a minimum of disturbances[11].

Inventory management is the responsibility of the Managing Director of a co-operative sugar factory. He performs this function with the help of two assistants, named as Stores-keeper and Godown-keeper. Store-keeper handles the stores of consumable items and godown-keeper looks after the stock of sugar. Separate premises are provided in the campus of factory to stores of consumable items and stock of sugar. Store ledgers are maintained separately for consumable stores and stock of sugar. Every receipt and issue is recorded in this ledger and balance of all items is kept update. Stock of stores and spares and stock of sugar, both are major items of inventory in co-operative sugar factories and these two items are handled by separate persons.

Inventory occupies a major share in working capital of co-operative sugar factories. On an average 80% to 90% of the amount of working capital of sugar factories is blocked in inventories. Major part of inventory is formed by stock of finished goods, i.e. sugar. So inventory management is crucial part of financial management of co-operative sugar factories.

Inventory of co-operative sugar factory includes the stock of work in progress, finished goods and stores and spares. Raw material inventory is not part of inventory as raw material is used for production, immediately after it is brought to factory. No stock of raw material is made in co-operative sugar factory. Sugarcane is the only raw material. It cannot be stored as the sugar content in sugarcane starts reducing as soon as it is harvested. Thus sugarcane is sent to production immediately, after it is harvested from farms.

Peculiar nature of sugarcane crop is that it starts losing the water content in it due to dry age, reducing thereby the juice contents in the plant and ultimately affecting sugar availability. During the process of dry age, the other chemical process of inversion of sucrose into glucose, and fructose also take place. The sucrose content is thus reduced, resulting in ultimate reduction in recovery of sugar from each cane crop. It has been estimated that dry age of cane crop for about 24 to 48 hours from its harvest time may result in 0.53 to 0.83 per cent reduction in recovery of sugar. Therefore, it becomes essential that sugarcane is available to sugar factory, within the shortest possible distance, in compact area, so that fully matured sugarcane is brought within minimum time loss between harvesting and crushing of sugarcane[12]. Because of this peculiar nature of sugarcane crop it cannot be stored and thus do not become a part of inventory. Hence there is no raw material inventory in co-operative sugar factories. Following are the components of inventory in co-operative sugar factories:

(i) Work in Process Inventory

Work in process is the goods in process of manufacture. In view of accounting, work in process is cost of raw material transferred plus wages and direct manufacturing expenses. The main item of work in process in co-operative sugar factories is raw sugar. In addition, molasses and bagasse are also taken as work in progress. The valuation of all items is made together as work in process.

(ii) Finished Good Inventory

Finished goods inventory is the stock of white sugar. This is the final product of sugar factory. Stock of sugar is valued at levy price and free price as per the quota sanctioned by Government to the particular factory.

(iii) Stores and Spares Inventory

Stores and spares inventory is consumable stores required by the co-operative sugar factory. Stores include stores for repairs and maintenance of plant and machinery, packing material, i.e. gunny bags, chemicals, cleaning materials, fuel and fuel stores, construction stores, iron and steel items, electrical goods stores, lab materials, medical stores, printing and stationary and all types of stores items. The stores is valued at purchase price and recorded in accounts.

Purchase of Sugarcane

Sugarcane is the main raw material of sugar factory. Purchase of sugarcane is important function in sugar factory. Sugarcane is a perishable raw material. It should be sent to production immediately after it is harvested. Harvesting programme is prepared by sugar factory and cane is brought to factory as per the requirement of production. To get fully matured and quality cane, schemes of cane development are implemented by sugar factories in its area of operation. Two expert officers named as Agriculture Development Officer and Cane Development Officer are appointed to look after the cane plantation, cane development and cane harvesting programme. The entire programme of cane plantation and cane harvesting are prepared well in advance for every season by these officers and cane purchases are made as this predetermined programme.

Purchase price of cane is fixed by the State Government for each factory, based upon the production cost and efficiency. This price must be always more than statutory minimum price fixed by Central Government and State Advisory Price, advised by State Government. Final purchase price of cane is paid after the crushing season is over, but first instalment is paid to farmers within fortnight of the harvesting of cane. The cane price paid by sugar factories studied ranges from Rs. 500 to Rs. 1100 per ton. It is observed that profit making factories paid relatively higher price than loss making factories.

Sale of Sugar

Sugar factories are not free to sell their sugar on their own, even though sugar industry is liberalised. Sale of sugar is regulated by central Government. Central Government regulates sales of sugar through release of quota for every three months to each factory. This is because Government regulates the supply of sugar to control its prices and to make uninterrupted supply to consumers. This is done by Government as the sugar comes under the Essential Commodities Act.

Presently, the policy adopted by Government is partial control, under which 15% of the production of sugar must be sold by every factory under 'Levy sugar quota,' and 85% under 'free quota'. Government purchases levy sugar at a lower price than market price and uses it for sale through public distribution system. 85% of the production of the sugar can be sold in free market at market price, but only under the release quota sanctioned. It was a common complaint of all co-operative sugar factories studied that this system of sales of sugar is costly as the sugar is not speedily sold and money blocked in stock of sugar is not realized. This results into shortage of cash and additional working capital loans are to be raised to meet the deficit cash. In addition, there is a huge production of sugar since last five years and so supply of sugar is more than its demand. This resulted into reduction of market prices of sugar. It will not be wrong to state that sales function of the co-operative sugar factory is totally influenced by government and sugar factory is helpless in this regard.

Growth of Inventories

Table 5.1 shows the growth of inventories in co-operative sugar factories studied. Growth is shown for every year for the study period of ten years from 1991-92 to 2000-01 for each factory.

For showing growth, growth indices are used. The base year taken to construct the indices is 1991-92.

In Aurangabad district, Sant Eknath showed increasing trend in growth of inventory except in the year 1993-94 and 1997-98. The maximum growth was 314% in 2000-01. It showed decreasing trend in the year 1993-94 and 1997-98 because factory was not in operation in these years and thus stock of sugar was at lower level. In Siddheshwar, except 1992-93 and 1997-98, there has been a continuous growth in inventory to the maximum of 354% in 2000-01.

In Jalna district, Jalna and Samarth showed continuous growth except in 1996-97 and 1997-98 in Jalna and 1992-93 and 1993-94 in Samarth. The maximum growth index was 151% in 2000-01 in Jalna and 621% in 2000-01 in Samarth. Jalna showed decrease in the year 1996-97 and 1997-98 because the factory was not in operation in these two years. Samarth also showed decrease in the year 1992-93 and 1993-94 because of lower production of sugar.

In Beed district, Gajanan showed upward and downward trends in the growth of inventories. The maximum growth index was 420% in 2000-01. Annual average index for ten years was 106% in Jai Bhavani also showed similar trends in the growth of inventory. The maximum growth index shown was 330% in the year 2000-01.

In Parbhani district, Godawari Dudhana showed up and downward trends in the growth of inventory. Maximum growth index was 184% in the year 2000-01. Purna showed continued growth throughout the period to the maximum of 349% in the year 2000-01.

In Nanded district, Shankar and Godawari Manar showed continuous growth in inventories except 1992-93 and 1997-98. This is because production of sugar was at lower level in these factories in the year 1992-93 and 1997-98 in comparison to the remaining years of study period. The maximum growth index was 282% in Shankar in 2000-01 and 293% in 1999-00 in Godawari Manar.

Table—5.1: Growth Indices of Inventories in Co-operative Factories Under Study

Sl.No.	Name of the Factory	91-92	92-93	93-94	94-95	95-96	96-97	97-98	98-99	99-00	00-01	Average
01.	Sant Eknath	100	98	11	119	137	111	51	153	199	314	129
02.	Siddheshwar	100	77	141	178	213	210	50	193	296	354	181
03.	Jalna	100	112	131	143	137	32	9	103	145	151	106
04.	Samarth	100	116	69	176	298	274	222	365	413	621	265
05.	Gajanan	100	37	20	133	122	81	38	182	235	420	137
06.	Jaibhavani	100	67	19	152	150	159	135	233	290	330	164
07.	Godawari Dudhana	100	117	64	158	160	88	59	100	122	184	115
08.	Purna	100	131	138	195	180	190	176	191	241	349	189
09.	Shankar	100	91	110	155	180	197	144	176	244	282	168
10.	Godawari Manar	100	103	146	195	241	298	68	239	293	384	207
11.	Jai Jawan	100	100	79	143	164	196	188	217	283	417	189
12.	Manjra	100	165	160	208	254	293	317	293	506	606	290
13.	Tuljabhavani	100	103	28	127	145	188	163	153	222	312	154
14.	Terna	100	71	60	164	190	209	235	264	410	578	228

Source: Annual reports of co-operative sugar factories under study from 1991-92 to 2000-01.

In Latur district, Jai Jawan Jai Kisan and Manjra Shetkari showed continuous growth in inventory. The maximum growth was 282% in 2000-01. In Jai Jawan Jai Kisan there has been a continuous growth in inventories to maximum 606% in 2000-01.

In Osmanabad district, Tuljabhavani Shetkari and Terna Shetkari showed the same pattern of growth in inventories, except 1993-94 and maximum growth index was 312% in Tuljabhavani and 578% in Terna Shetkari.

Table 5.1 shows that growth indices in 2500 TCD factories like Siddheshwar, Samarth, Jai Bhavani, Purna Manjra and Terna are more than remaining 1250 TCD factories. Growth indices are comparatively high in Latur and Osmanabad district than other districts, Samarth shows the highest growth of inventory at 621% in 2000-01 and Jalna showed the lowest growth of inventory at 9% in 1997-98. All factories showed lower growth in 1993-94 and in 1997-98, due to low production.

Adequacy of Inventory—Inventory Turn over Ratios

Inventory turnover ratio is also known as stock turnover ratio in the traditional language. It helps in determining the liquidity of a firm as much as it gives the rate which inventories are converted into sales than into cash. It assists the financial manager in evaluating inventory policy to avoid any danger of over-stocking.

Inventory turnover is an indication of the velocity with which merchandise moves through the business. An inventory turnover ratio, standing itself, means absolutely nothing, because there is no fixed norm for inventory, which depends greatly in the nature of the industry and on the sale policies followed by the firm[13].

Inventory is the most important factor in working capital. It constitutes major portion of current assets. Inventory turnover ratio is also known as stock turnover ratio. It expresses the relationship between cost of goods and average inventory for the given period. Any abatement in turnover would disturb the financial structure and soundness of the factory. To evaluate working capital, it is necessary to analyse the efficiency of inventory management by its turnover ratio[14]. It helps to decide whether the investment in inventory is used efficiently or not. There is no fixed norm for inventory turnover. Mostly, it depends on nature of the firm and sales policies adopted by them.

Formulation :

$$\text{Inventory turnover ratio} = \frac{\text{Cost of goods sold}}{\text{Net sales}}$$

or

$$\frac{\text{Sales}}{\text{Average inventory}}$$

Adequacy of the inventories can be known by using inventory turnover ratio. More the ratio, more the efficiency of inventory management, and less the ratio, less the efficiency is taken as norms. It has been the experience of co-operative sugar factories that they hold excess inventory of finished goods or stores and spares. Out of the fourteen factories studied not a single factory found any deficit of inventory. No shortage of either finished goods or stores and spares inventory is found in the factories studied. Table 5.2 shows inventory turnover ratio of co-operative sugar factories studied. Ratios are computed for every year from 1991-92 to 2000-01. The ratio is computed by using the formula sales divided by average inventory. The average inventory is calculated as opening stock of inventory plus closing stock of inventory divided by two. This ratio shows the operation of working capital.

Factory-wise Inventory Turnover Ratio

In Aurangabad district, it can be observed from the Table 5.2 that the average inventory turnover ratio of Sant Eknath was 1.10:1. Highest inventory turnover ratio recorded was 1.38 in 1991-92. It is not favourable position for the factory. The lowest ratio registered in 1997-98 was 0.58; no doubt it is red signal for the factory.

The average inventory turnover ratio in Siddheshwar observed was 1.35:1. Highest inventory turnover ratio recorded was 1.96 in 1991-92. It was a favourable position for the factory to some extent. The lowest ratio ascertained was 0.91 in 1996-97, expressing huge stock of inventory. It indicates that factory has maintained huge stock of sugar, blocking heavy amount, and thus affecting the liquidity position of the factory.

Table—5.2: Inventory Turnover Ratio of Co-operative Sugar Factories Under Study

Sl.No.	Name of Factory	91-92	92-93	93-94	94-95	95-96	96-97	97-98	98-99	99-00	00-01	Average
01.	Sant Eknath	1.38	1.17	0.88	0.61	1.47	1.14	0.58	1.37	1.27	1.16	1.10
02.	Siddheshwar	1.96	1.95	1.03	1.15	1.38	0.91	1.35	1.51	1.32	0.94	1.35
03.	Jalna	1.61	1.36	1.49	1.04	1.25	1.46	1.18	1.61	1.20	0.81	1.30
04.	Samarth	1.73	1.41	1.52	0.74	1.00	1.19	0.69	1.21	1.21	1.16	1.19
05.	Gajanan	2.14	1.05	0.64	0.62	1.40	1.20	0.81	1.08	1.06	1.18	1.12
06.	Jaibhavani	1.49	1.54	1.20	0.54	1.26	0.97	0.82	1.24	1.01	1.09	1.12
07.	Godawari Dudhana	1.56	1.27	1.07	0.39	0.86	1.10	0.90	0.47	0.73	0.88	0.92
08.	Purna	1.36	1.30	1.47	0.90	1.19	1.12	1.06	1.17	0.91	0.79	1.13
09.	Shankar	1.89	1.88	1.38	1.01	1.18	1.10	1.03	1.11	0.91	0.77	1.23
10.	Godawari Manar	1.66	1.54	1.08	1.06	1.12	1.00	0.51	1.39	1.03	1.03	1.14
11.	Jai Jawan	1.48	1.17	1.34	0.86	1.29	1.06	0.96	1.11	1.06	0.96	1.13
12.	Manjra	1.92	1.37	1.41	1.29	1.38	1.07	1.12	1.57	1.28	1.18	1.36
13.	Tuljabhavani	1.60	1.30	1.90	0.60	1.17	0.94	0.84	1.01	1.32	0.94	1.16
14.	Terna	1.34	1.39	1.12	0.69	1.24	1.15	1.04	1.28	1.25	1.04	1.15
	Industry Average	1.65	1.40	1.25	0.82	1.22	1.10	0.92	1.22	1.11	0.99	1.17

Source: Annual reports of co-operative sugar factories under study from 1991-92 to 2000-01.

In Jalna district, the average inventory turnover ratio in Jalna ascertained was 1.30:1 indicating excessive inventory level than warranted by production. It is clear that high inventory turnover ratio assumed favourable sales. However, low inventory turnover ratio blocks the fund unnecessarily in inventory, making an adverse effect on working capital or liquidity position of the firm. Highest inventory turnover ratio or 1.61 was recorded in 1991-92 and 1998-99 due to low-level inventory and increased sales volume. It is clear that restriction of the Government on sale of sugar results in an augmented total inventory. Hence, maximum stock of inventory can never be positive point for the factory.

The average inventory turnover ratio in Samarth for the desired period was 1.19:1. High inventory turnover ratio may be appreciable, however, there is no standard ratio. The lowest inventory turnover ratio ascertained was 0.69, imitating huge amount of inventory against sales. It indicates poor performance of inventory management. Huge stock of inventory blocks heavy amount of cash. It becomes difficult to meet short-term obligations. The highest ratio was 1.73 in 1991-92, because of low inventory and increased sales volume. It indicates efficient control over inventory.

The average inventory turnover ratio in Gajanan was observed 1.12:1. Highest inventory turnover ratio recorded was 2.14 in 1991-92 due to higher sales volume. It was favourable position for the factory to some extent. The lowest ratio was registered in 1994-95 expressing higher amount of inventory. The ratio observed below 1 in six years of the study period. It indicates that factory has maintained huge stock of inventory and thus affecting the liquidity position of the factory.

The average inventory turnover ratio in Jaibhavani was the same as in Gajanan, i.e. 1.12:1. The highest inventory turnover ratio provides greater credit for the factory, however, there is no standard ratio. The lowest inventory turnover ratio ascertained was 0.54 in 1994-95, reflecting huge amount of inventory against sales. It indicates poor performance of the factory. The highest ratio was 1.54 in 1992-93, because of low inventory as compared to other components of ratio. It can be seen from the table that factory maintained the inventory turnover ratio below 1.10 in 5 years of the study period.

The average inventory turnover ratio in Godawari Dudhana observed was 0.92:1, which is lowest among all sugar factories studied. The highest ratio ascertained was 1.56 in 1991-92, due to increased sales volume. It seems good position for the factory. In remaining years of the study period, the ratio was very weak. It is found below 1.00, in 6 years of the study period. It shows inefficient control over inventory. The huge amount of inventory creates severe crunch in short-term liquidity.

Purna showed average inventory turnover ratio of 1.13:1 for the given period, which is lower than the average of Marathwada region. The highest inventory turnover ratio recorded was 1.47 in 1993-94, due to increased sales volume. It was a favourable position for the factory to some extent. The lowest ratio ascertained was 0.79 in 2000-01, intimating the huge amount of inventory against sales. It indicates poor performance of the factory. It may be observed that the factory has failed in proper and efficient control over inventory.

From the table it may be ascertained that average inventory turnover ratio of Shankar was 1.23:1, which is lower than the average of Marathwada region. The highest ratio recorded was 1.89 in 1991-92, due to greater sales volume and smaller inventory. It indicates satisfactory position of the factory, to some extent. The lowest ratio registered was 0.77 in 2000-01 because of the huge amount of inventory. It leads to unworthy financial position. The ratio observed below 1.10 in 3 years of the study period. It indicates poor control over inventory. No doubt, it is red signal for the factory.

Table 5.2 indicates that the average inventory turnover ratio in Godawari Manar for the study period was 1.14:1. High inventory turnover ratio may be appreciable, however, there is no standard ratio. The highest ratio observed was 1.66 in 1991-92, because of low inventory and increased sales volume. The ratio showed much fluctuations during the study period. The lowest ratio ascertained was 0.51 in 1997-98 reflecting the huge stock of inventory and lower amount of sales. It indicates poor inventory management.

The average inventory turnover ratio of Jai Jawan Jai Kisan for given period was 1.13:1, which was less than the average of Marathwada region. The highest ratio ascertained was 1.48 in 1991-92, due to increased sales volume and low stock of inventory. This may be better position for the factory. The lowest inventory turnover ratio observed was 0.96 in 1997-98, intimating the huge amount of inventory against decreased sales volume. The lowest inventory turnover indicates the inability to augment sales. It is clear that the factory has maintained huge stock of finished goods blocking heavy amount.

From the Table 5.2 it may be observed that the average inventory turnover ratio of Manjra was 1.36:1, which is highest among all sugar factories studied. The higher inventory turnover ratio provides greater credit for the factory. The highest ratio recorded was 1.92 in 1991-92, due to smaller amount of inventory. Most of the sugar factories studied, show highest inventory turnover ratio in 1991-92. It showed favourable position for all the factories studied.

The ratio of Manjra was 1.07:1 in the year 1996-97 because low sales and higher amount of inventory. It leads to unworthy financial position. It indicates poor control over the inventory. It is clear that huge amount of inventory requires tremendous investment and thus it affects the financial position of the factory. It may also result in inability of the factory in meeting the short-term obligations. Hence, proper and efficient control over the inventory needed.

The average inventory turnover ratio in Tuljabhavani for the study period was 1.16:1. Highest inventory turnover ratio was 1.60 in 1991-92, reflecting higher sales volume. It was a favourable position for the factory to some extent. The lowest ratio ascertained was 0.60 in 1994-95, intimating little amount of sale. The ratio was observed below 1 in three years of the study period. It was unfavourable position for the factory. Low inventory turnover ratio indicates inability of the factory to increase sales; huge amount unduly tied up with inventory. It may affect the financial position of the factory.

The average inventory turnover ratio observed in Terna was 1.15:1. Highest ratio appeared was 1.34 in 1991-92 and lowest ratio ascertained 0.69 in 1994-95. It was not favourable position for the factory. The ratio observed below 1.10 in three years of the study period. The low inventory turnover ratio indicates inability to augment the sales. It is clear that the factory has maintained huge stock of finished goods, blocking heavy amount. Expedient sales policy could definitely help in controlling the inventory but also strengthening the ratio. Excessive amount will not tie up in the inventory and it will helpful in uplifting the factory in all respect.

It may be observed from the Table 5.2 that not a single factory touched the ratio of 2:1. It is clear that the factories have maintained huge stock of finished goods and thus blocking heavy amount. It is common feature of sugar factories that they have to hold huge stock of sugar continuously for a long period. Hence, it is recommended that the factories should formulate suitable sales policies to encash the inventory, and Government should help the factories in augmenting the sales volume.

Fig. 5 (a) shows the inventory turnover ratio of the sugar factories studied.

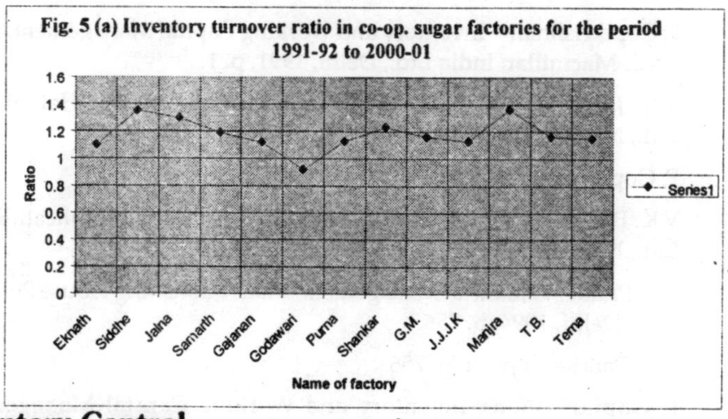

Fig. 5 (a) Inventory turnover ratio in co-op. sugar factories for the period 1991-92 to 2000-01

Inventory Control

Various techniques are available for the control of inventories. But except classification and codification no other techniques of control for inventories are used by co-operative sugar factories studied. Finished goods and consumable stores are the major components of inventories in co-operative sugar factories. It is found that both the components were beyond the control of management by co-operative sugar factories.

Regarding finished goods inventory, that is stock of sugar, the co-operative sugar factories are helpless. They cannot speed up sales and cannot reduce this inventory through sales. They cannot control production of sugar as to reduce the excess finished goods inventory because they have to crush every stock of cane in their area of operation considering it as their social responsibility. This means both the important functions, production and sales, are beyond the control of sugar factories.

Classification and codification of consumable stores items are made in all factories studied. All items classification and codifications are numerical and alphabetical in nature. It has been found that no other control measures, like fixation of minimum level, maximum level, order level and economic order quantity, are used by sugar factories studied. Physical verification of stock is made, but casually and not regularly. Bin card and store ledgers are used by all sugar factories studied.

REFERENCES

1. P. Gopikrishnan—Inventory and Working Capital Management, Hand Book-Macmillan India Ltd., Delhi, 1991, p. 1.
2. John J. Hampton—Financial Decision Making, Prentice Hall of India Ltd., New Delhi, 1980, p. 244.
3. P. Gopikrishnan— op. cit. p. 1.
4. V.K. Bhalla—Working Capital Management, Anmol Publication Pvt. Ltd., New Delhi, 1998, p. 353.
5. I.M. Pande—Financial Management, Vikas Publishing House Pvt. Ltd., New Delhi, 1994, p. 756.
6. I.M. Pande— op. cit. p. 756.
7. P. Gopikrishnan—Inventory and Working Capital Management, Handbook, Macmillan India Ltd., Delhi-1991, p. 128.
8. Lammer Lee Jr. and Donald W. Dobler—Purchasing and Material Management, Tata McGraw-Hill Publishing Co. Ltd., New Delhi, 1978, p. 188.

9. S.C. Baradia—Working Capital Management, Pointer Publisher, Jaipur, 1988, p. 82.
10. National Council of Applied Economic Research, New Delhi—Structure of Working Capital, 1966, p. 11.
11. Lowrence J. Gitman—Principles of Management Finance, Harper & Row Publishers, New York, 1976, p. 213.
12. Kharchae R. M. —Sugar Co-operatives in Developing Economy, Parimal Prakashan, Aurangabad, 1989, p. 104.
13. Man Mohan Goyal—Principles of Management Accounting, Sahitya Bhavan, Agra, 1990, pp. 429-30.
14. Sharma N.K. —Financial Management and Appraisal, Arihant Publishing House, Jaipur, 1994, p. 150.

6

Receivable Management

Introduction

Receivable is an important component of working capital. It occupies the second important place after inventories and constitutes a substantial portion of current assets. Receivables arise through credit sales and credit sale is considered to be an important marketing tool, acting as a bridge for the movement of goods from production and distribution stages to customers finally. Credit sales are made to maintain and to increase sales. Selling on credit is easy but recoveries from receivables are difficult which may ultimately lead to cash crunch. Thus receivable management occupies important place in working capital management.

Account receivables have a significant part in the working capital of the business next to inventories. They are related to trade credit, which has become an essential marketing tool in modern business. When firm sells goods for cash, payments are received immediately and therefore no receivables are created. However, when firm sells goods or services on credit, the payments are postponed to further dates and receivables are created. Usually credit sales are made on open accounts, which mean that no formal acknowledgement of debt obligation is taken from buyers. The only document of evidence is a purchase order or invoice.

Selling on credit is an easy job, but recovery from customers is a delicate job. While recovering the amount from the customers promptly. Prompt recoveries from customers without hurting their relations is a central idea of receivable management. The firm should keep in mind its long term relationship with the customers.

Objectives of Maintaining Receivables

Account receivables play a major role in the conduct of business. Most of the firms do not demand cash from customers immediately on sales as to show their trust in the credit worthiness of customers. Customer also expect the same from seller as to finance their deficit cash conveniently without harming their trustworthiness. This mutual understanding is the main reason of maintaining accounts receivables. In brief the objectives of maintaining receivables are as follows[1].

(a) ***Expansion of Sales:*** Customers are encouraged for purchases with the offer of credit. So for sales expansion receivables are maintained.

(b) ***Maintaining Liquidity:*** The concept of operating cycle explains the fact that receivables are one step ahead of inventories. So, for facilitating liquidity, credit sales are preferred than inventories.

(c) ***Increase in Profits:*** When credit is offered, sales are increased which results into increase in profit. A firm maintains receivables and tries to earn more profit.

(d) ***Meeting Competitions:*** A firm may have to resort to granting of credit facilities to its customers because of similar facilities being granted by competing firms to avoid the loss of sales from customers who would buy elsewhere if they did not receive the expected credit.

The nature of sugar industry is different from other industries. The co-operative sugar factories do not allow credit sales. The sale of sugar is always made in cash and no credit is granted in any case. As there are no credit sales, no question arises about determination of credit policy.

The level of firm's account receivables is determined by volume of its sales and average collection periods[2]. The relative size of investment of company in accounts recievables depends upon industry in which it operates, its credit policy and its sales volume[3].

Function of Receivables Management

The major function of receivables management is to keep a balance between risk and returns related to receivables. This function is performed through different stages, which are discussed below:

(i) ***Determining Credit Policy:*** For efficient management of receivables a firm must determine a credit policy. While determining firm's credit policy, certain factors are to be considered, which are: (a) Credit standard; (b) Credit terms; (c) Collection efforts; (d) Optimum credit policy; and (e) Allocation of authority related to credit.

(a) ***Credit Standards:*** Credit standards are the criteria that determine what customers will be granted credit and to what extent[4]. The size of receivables will be high when credit standards are loose and it will be small when credit standards are tight. The credit standards must not be more loose or more tight. Both loose and tight standards have adverse impact on profitability of receivables.

(b) ***Credit Terms:*** Credit terms refer to the terms under which a firm sells goods on credit to its customers. Two components of credit terms are (i) credit period; and (ii) cash discount.

(c) ***Collection Effort and Policies:*** Collection policy refers to the procedures the firm uses to collect past accounts. Collection policy is necessary to speed up the collections from slow payers and avoid bad debts. Standard collection procedures include sending out letters, making phone calls, turning over the account to an outside collection agency and instigating lawsuits. The collection procedure may be expensive in terms of both out of pocket costs and cost of goodwill.

(d) ***Optimum Credit Policy:*** While designing the credit policy costs and benefits of all these variables are to be considered individually and jointly to find their integrated impact over the goal of maximisation of profit. The term profit is expressed in different ways thus goal of credit policy is not only maximisation of profit but the maximisation of value.

(e) ***Allocation of Authority and Responsibility:*** The function of receivable management is concerned with two departments, viz. sales department and finance department. There may be conflict between finance department and sales department, as the finance department will suggest a tight credit policy while sales department will suggest a loose credit policy. To avoid these conflicts and confusions there should be a clear definition of authority as to who will grant credit and as to who will be responsible for collections. This will facilitate the receivables management.

(ii) ***Implementation of Policy:*** For effective management of receivables a firm should lay down clear-cut credit procedures. Credit procedure may vary from customer to customer. Every credit should be sanctioned only through the credit procedures laid down by the firm. Credit procedure involves the following steps:

(i) Obtaining information about applicant;

(ii) Analysing information;

(iii) Credit decision.

(iii) ***Control of Receivables:*** The important function of receivables management is to control receivables. Formulation of optimum credit policy is itself a technique of controlling receivables. But taking into consideration huge number of accounts receivables and their varied types of behaviour, use of additional control techniques becomes necessary. Control of receivables involves the following:

***Continuous Review, Follow up and Collections*:** For controlling receivables and decreasing average collection period and bad debts, constant review of the receivables should be taken and follow up for collection should be continuously made. For this separate committee may formed consisting of personnel of finance and sales departments. The committee will meet weekly, fortnightly or monthly and will take a review of receivables position and initiate necessary actions for collections.

Nature and Components of Receivables in Co-operative Sugar Factories

Receivables are second most important segment of working capital next to inventory. Though investment in receivables in co-operative sugar factories is less, the risks related to receivables are high. So careful analysis and proper management of receivables are essential. Accounts receivables represent the amount due from customers, as a result of selling goods on credit. In accounting terms receivables are taken in broad sense as the 'amount receivables' not only for credit sales, but also for other transactions like advance paid to employees and suppliers, claims for expenses, accrued non-trading incomes and sundry amounts receivable.

In co-operative sugar factories, the concept of 'Receivables' is altogether different from what is established. Co-operative sugar factories in Marathwada do not allow credit sales. The sale of sugar is always made in cash. In fact there is no need of making credit sales as the product is in great demand and totally controlled by Government. Sugar is sold by two ways in the co-operative sugar factories. First, the levy quota of sugar which is sold to State Government. It is purchased through district supply officer of all districts from the co-operative sugar factories in the relevant district. Second, the free sales quota of sugar which is sold in open market by inviting tenders. The free sale quota sugar can be sold in India or abroad. The important thing to be noted is that both the cases sales are made strictly in cash and no credit is granted. So the 'Account Receivables' due to credit sales do not exist in co-operative sugar factories. As there are no credit sales, no question arises about determination of credit policy, recovery from debtors, measures for speedy recoveries and doubtful debts and bad debts.

The treatment in sales of sugar is the same in co-operatives as well as private sugar factories.

There are receivables in co-operative sugar factories, not against credit sales, but against advances to employees, harvesting and transportation contractors, repairs and maintenance contractors, loans to farmers under various agricultural development schemes, prepaid expenses and deposits for central excise and others. There are few receivables against the credit sales of by-products like molasses, pressmud and bagasse. But these carry very few amounts as these by-products are also sold on cash terms. It will be better to make a list of components of receivables to understand it. The list as follows:

(i) Loans and advances to employees against salary;

(ii) Advances to harvesting and transportation contractors;

(iii) Advances to repairs and maintenance contractor for maintenance of plant and machinery;

(iv) Loans and advances to farmers for cane development, irrigation facilities, fertilizers, purchase of tractors, agricultural equipments, etc.;

(v) Deposits for central excise, electricity, etc.;

(vi) Prepaid expenses like insurance of plant and machinery and godowns.

The major share in receivables is contributed by advances to harvesting and transportation contractors. Other components occupy relatively less share. In co-operative sugar factory there are account receivables. But its different nature should be noted while analysing receivables management in co-operative sugar factory.

Recovery of Receivables

All components of receivables are easily recoverable, except advances to harvesting and transportation contractors. Loans and advances given to employees are recovered through their salary as per the factory regulations. So no question arises about the recovery. Advances to repairs and maintenance contractors are recovered from their bills promptly. Even some factories keep their bill outstanding for long periods. So no problem of recovery of these advances is faced. Loans and advances to farmers are recovered from their sugarcane bills. Prepaid expenses and deposits are recovered in course of activity of the factory.

It is observed in the sugar factories studied that there are some problems of recovery of advances given to harvesting and transportation contractors. The written contract for harvesting is made with labour contractor and advances up to 20% to 25% of his remuneration are given to him. No security is taken from labour contractor except documents of his agricultural land, if holds any. If contractor makes default in harvesting job, it becomes difficult to control him and to recover the advances given to him. Because of increasing demand for harvesting labour due to growth in sugar factories, labour problem became serious. Sometimes contractors take advances from more than one factory and could not manage the supply of cane. Sometimes contractors could not collect sufficient labour and so cannot work efficiently. All these factors create problems, in supply of sugarcane and recovery of harvesting advance. Advances given to bullock carts, tractors and trucks are recovered easily as their vehicles are mortgaged with the sugar factory.

Organisation for Receivables Management

The picture of receivables management is altogether different in co-operative sugar factories, because the nature of receivables is different in these factories. No credit sales are permitted in sugar factories. So receivables management in co-operative sugar factories does not include credit policies, collection policies and optimum level of investment in receivables. All these variables are considered in co-operative sugar factories not in relation to credit sales but in relation to loans and advances to farmers and contractors.

Receivable management in co-operative sugar factories is 'the formulation of policy regarding advances to farmers, harvesting and transportation contractors, repairs and maintenance contractors and employees as to manage the crushing season efficiently'. The major components of receivables in sugar factories are advances to harvesting and transportation contractors. It is observed in the co-operative sugar factories that policies regarding the advances to be given to the contractors are determined by board of directors. Responsibility is not assigned to any officer and decision is taken by board itself. This is for reasons, firstly, issuing advances and making recovery is a risky job, so an officer generally tends to work as per instructions of higher authority and not at his own. Secondly, the harvesting and transportation contractors are generally known to directors as the directors used to be the farmers of the area. It came to know from the oral discussion with the officer of the factory that the directors are interested in sanctioning higher advances to harvesting and transportation contractors. While taking decision about the sanction of advances to contractors, the expert opinion of Managing Director, Agricultural Officer, Cane Development Officer are considered, but decision is taken by board of directors in its meeting.

All advances are recovered from the bills of concerned contractors. In terms of management, the responsibility of receivable management is entirely upon managing director of the factory and he performs it with the help of officers of the related section. Necessary securities are taken while giving all types of advances. Necessary documents and vouchers are prepared, entries made, details are recorded and recovery is made in due course.

Growth of Receivables

The growing tendency of receivables in the co-operative sugar factories studied is shown in Table 6.1. The growth is shown for the period of ten years from 1991-92 to 2000-01 year-wise. It is shown with the help of growth index for which 1991-92 has been taken as base year.

In Sant Eknath, during the study period from 1991-92 to 2000-01, the receivables registered a rising trend as compared to the base year. The total receivables varied from Rs. 287.95 lakhs in 1991-92 to Rs. 751.20 lakhs in 2000-01. The growth index ranges between 100% in 1991-92 to 275% in 2000-01.

In Siddheshwar, growth index of receivables registered fluctuating trends during the study period. The lowest growth index observed was 84% in 1992-93, due to little amount of receivables, and highest index 323% in 1999-2000, due to high amount of receivables. This reveals that loan and advances were under control in the year 1992-93. It showed poor control over receivables in 1999-2000. The size of receivables varied from Rs. 205.05 lakhs to Rs. 788.95 lakhs.

In Jalna, the size of receivables and growth index registered fluctuating trends. The size of receivables varied from Rs. 204.18 lakhs in 1992-93 to Rs. 491.39 lakhs in 1999-2000. The growth index ranges from 84% in 1992-93 to 202% in 1999-2000, which is considerably lower than Siddheshwar. It showed good control over receivables during the study period. It is observed that the receivables showed downward trend in 2000-01.

The average growth trend of receivables in Samarth was observed 177%, which is significantly higher than Jalna. It showed fluctuating trends during the study period. The growth index ranges from 73% in 1992-93 to 340% in 2000-01. It is observed that the factory had efficient control over receivables in first three years of the study period. Thereafter it showed higher index of receivables. The highest index observed was 340% in 2000-01. It reveals the poor control over receivables management. It indicates that the factory has failed in controlling receivables.

In Gajanan, the average growth index observed was 219%, which is higher than Samarth. The lowest index ascertained was 91% in 1992-93. The size of receivables was also lowest in that year. The highest growth index appeared was 482% in 2000-01. It indicates a higher amount of receivables. Continuous increasing trend was observed from 1995-96 to 2000-01. It indicates inefficient control over receivables.

In Jaibhavani, the average growth index observed was 205%, which is slightly lower than Gajanan. The lowest growth index appeared was 68% in 1994-95, expressing little amount of receivables. It indicates good control over receivables. The highest growth index registered was 355% in 1999-2000, which express the unsatisfactory position of the receivables.

Table—6.1: Growth Indices of Receivables in Co-operative Sugar Factories Under Study

Sl.No.	*Name of Factory*	*91-92*	*92-93*	*93-94*	*94-95*	*95-96*	*96-97*	*97-98*	*98-99*	*99-00*	*00-01*	*Average*
01.	Sant Eknath	100	122	137	130	136	160	171	169	202	275	160
02.	Siddheshwar	100	84	92	202	223	234	283	261	323	285	209
03.	Jalna	100	84	120	175	103	119	110	149	202	132	129
04.	Samarth	100	73	105	186	171	178	176	162	279	340	177
05.	Gajanan	100	91	187	207	114	171	154	278	405	482	219
06.	Jaibhavani	100	83	167	68	118	227	278	340	355	312	205
07.	Godawari Dudhana	100	139	221	222	351	856	272	457	119	550	329
08.	Purna	100	107	52	83	79	82	111	96	103	88	90
09.	Shankar	100	91	106	125	100	99	114	160	245	209	135
10.	Godawari Manar	100	113	168	126	131	141	191	212	250	289	172
11.	Jai Jawan	100	65	91	90	100	113	138	139	133	151	102
12.	Manjra	100	73	143	128	129	232	306	352	269	452	208
13.	Tuljabhavani	100	90	147	155	204	213	244	265	222	229	177
14.	Terna	100	110	118	268	298	302	449	382	585	1373	388

Source: Annual reports of co-op. sugar factories from 1991-92 to 2000-01.

In Godawari Dudhana, the average growth index observed was 329%, which is considerably higher than the remaining factories under study. It indicates poor control over receivables. The lowest index ascertained was 100% in 1991-92 and highest 856% in 1996-97, due to higher amount of receivables. Thereafter it showed downward trend, but very much higher than the base year. In 2000-01 the growth index observed was 550%, stating inefficient control over receivables. It indicates inefficient collection policy and poor receivables management.

The average growth index observed in Purna was 90% which is lowest among all factories studied. The size of receivables varied from Rs. 786.77 in 1991-92 to Rs. 877.23 in 1997-98. The average growth index was observed lower due to high amount of receivables in base year, i.e. 1991-92. The lowest growth index appeared was 52% in 1993-94, due to low amount of receivables. The highest growth index ascertained was 111% in 1997-98. It indicates higher amount of receivables.

In Shankar, the average growth index observed was 135%, which is higher than Purna. The factory registered fluctuating growth trends during the study period. The lowest index observed was 91% in 1992-93 and highest 245% in 1999-2000. The growth trend observed below 100% in four years of the study period. It indicates a satisfactory position of receivables.

In Godawari Manar, the average growth index was observed was 172%, which is slightly higher than Shankar. The growth index ranges from 100% in 1991-92 to 289% in 2000-01. It registered continuous increasing trends from 1994-95 to 2000-01 during the study period. The size of receivables varied from Rs. 287.31 lakhs in 1991-92 to Rs. 830.63 lakhs in 2000-01. It showed increasing trends as compared to base year 1991-92.

The average growth index of receivables in Jai Jawan Jai Kisan observed was 114%, which is slightly lower than Shankar and Godawari Manar. It indicates good control over receivables during the study period. The lowest index appeared was 65% in 1992-93 and highest 170% in 2000-01. It registered fluctuating trends during the study period. The factory had its growth index of receivables, below 100% in three years of the study period. It indicates satisfactory performance of receivables.

In Manjra, the size of receivables varied from Rs. 186.37 lakhs in 1991-92 to Rs. 1161.58 lakhs in 2000-01. The average growth index observed was 208%, which is significantly higher than Jai Jawan Jai Kisan. The lowest index ascertained was 73% in 1992-93 and highest 452% in 2000-01. Growth index of the factory showed many fluctuations during the study period.

In Tuljabhavani, the average growth index of receivables ascertained was 177%, which is lower than Manjra. It also registered fluctuating trends during the study period. The lowest index of 90% was observed in 1992-93, due to lower amount of receivables. The highest growth index appeared was 265% in 1998-99. It may be observed that majority of the factories studied showed lowest index in 1992-93 and highest in 2000-01. However, Tuljabhavani showed highest index in 1998-99. Thereafter it showed decreasing trends. It indicates improvement in collection of receivables in last two years of the study period.

The average growth index in Terna was 388%, which is highest among all factories under study. It indicates poor control over receivables. The growth index ranges from 100% in 1991-92 to 1373% in 2000-01. The index was observed highest, i.e. 1373%, in 2000-01, due to huge amount of receivables. It indicates inefficient collection policy and poor receivables management. It may be observed that the factory had failed in efficient control of receivables.

The review of all amounts of receivables in sugar factories studied, show that the size of receivables is higher in 2500 TCD factories than 1250 TCD factories. It is observed from the sugar factories studied that the size of receivables is determined by the amount of advances given to harvesting and transportation contractors and farmers.

The table shows that the index of receivables in all factories has been growing year-by-year throughout the study period. All factories showed varied size of receivables, which is unexpected because of same type of schemes and pattern for granting loans and advances to farmers and contractors implemented in almost all factories studied. The size of receivables may vary in proportion to production, but it was not observed so. This shows in efficient control over receivables exercised by sugar factories.

Account Receivables Turnover Ratio

The efficiency of receivables management can be examined by finding receivables turnover ratio. Higher the ratio, higher the performing receivables management, and lower the ratio, lower will be the performance. In fact, receivables turnover ratio may not be much useful in examining the efficiency of the receivables management as in sugar factories, receivables do not contain debtors against credit sales. However, the receivables may be related with sales for analysis purposes as they contribute significant role in production and ultimately in sales. The account receivables turnover ratio of the sugar factories studied for the period from 1991-92 to 2000-01 is shown in Table. 6.2.

Factory-wise Receivables Turnover Ratio

In Aurangabad district, the average receivables turnover ratio in Sant Eknath observed 4 times of sales expressing the inefficiency of receivables management. The lowest ratio appeared was 1.40 times in 1994-95 denoting decrease in sales and increase in receivables. It showed very weak performance of receivables. Highest ratio recorded was 6.56 times in 1991-92, due to lower amount of receivables. It is observed that only in two years of the study period the factory showed ratio more than 5 times. This reveals inefficient collection policy. It indicates that factory was not able to collect the receivables within short period.

The average receivables turnover ratio observed in Siddheshwar was 8 times of sales expressing the efficiency of receivables management. It showed good performance of receivables. The lowest ratio ascertained was 4.28 times, reflecting increase in receivables. The highest ratio enlisted was 12.47 times in 1991-92 reflecting lower amount of receivables and increase in sales. It indicates the ability of factory in meeting the short-term obligations.

In Jalna district, Jalna SSK showed the average receivables turnover ratio 7 times of sales which was quite more than the average of Marathwada region, i.e. 6 per cent. The factory showed satisfactory receivables turnover ratio during the first two years of the study period. Thereafter it showed fluctuating trend throughout the study period. The lowest ratio ascertained was 1.35 times, reflecting decrease in sales with no significant change in receivables. This reveals that the sale of sugar has decreased due to off season of the factory and receivables were not proportionately decreased. The ratio indicates poor receivables management. The highest ratio enlisted was 12.47 times in 1991-92 expressing increase in sales. Thereafter it showed decrease in the ratio throughout the study period.

The average receivables turnover ratio observed in Samarth was 8 times, which is higher than the average of Marathwada region. It indicates good performance of receivables. The lowest ratio appeared was 3.27 times, reflecting decrease in sales. It shows that the factory has failed in controlling the receivables. Hence, its short-term financial position seems to be unsatisfactory. The ratio shows much fluctuation during the study period from 1991-92 to 2000-01. The highest ratio recorded was 11.08 times in 1999-2000, expressing satisfactory performance of receivables. It shows the ratio above 7 times in seven years of the study period.

In Beed district, the average receivables turnover ratio observed in Gajanan was 5 timesof sales. The factory showed satisfactory receivables turnover ratio in 1991-92 and 1992-93. Thereafter it showed fluctuating trend throughout the study period. The lowest ratio appeared was 0.91 in 1993-94. It reflects decrease in sales and no significant change in the size of receivables. It reveals that the sale of sugar has decreased due to off crushing season of the factory, but receivables were not proportionately decreased. It indicates poor control over the receivables. It is observed that the receivables turnover ratio was less than 6 times in 8 years of the study period. This clears that factory failed in efficient control over receivables.

The average receivables turnover ratio in Jaibhavani observed was 7 times of sales, which is slightly higher than the average of Marathwada region. It indicates satisfactory performance of receivables to some extent. The lowest ratio appeared was 2.69 in 1994-95 expressing lower sales volume. The amount of receivables did not change in proportion to sales. A lower ratio of 2.87 was

Table—6.2: Receivable Turnover Ratios in Co-op. Sugar Factories Under Study

Sl.No.	Name of the Factory	91-92	92-93	93-94	94-95	95-96	96-97	97-98	98-99	99-00	00-01	Average
01.	Sant Eknath	6.56	4.98	3.33	1.40	3.95	4.67	1.70	2.77	5.76	6.18	4
02.	Siddheshwar	12.47	11.93	7.94	7.82	8.07	5.36	4.33	4.28	7.04	6.37	8
03.	Jalna	10.33	10.01	11.24	6.13	8.07	7.12	1.35	4.47	5.41	4.58	7
04.	Samarth	9.10	9.28	4.16	3.27	7.01	10.26	5.06	11.08	11.22	10.14	8
05.	Gajanan	13.30	4.69	0.91	1.62	6.89	5.33	1.87	4.35	3.90	5.44	5
06.	Jaibhawani	10.23	9.71	2.87	2.69	14.04	6.04	3.29	5.10	5.22	7.00	7
07.	Godawari	9.41	6.92	3.21	1.96	7.81	4.24	1.40	0.65	1.24	2.16	4
08.	Purna	3.25	3.47	5.90	4.39	6.61	5.08	4.66	4.95	4.70	5.79	5
09.	Shankar	5.99	5.94	4.44	3.68	5.58	6.63	5.27	4.13	3.00	2.83	5
10.	Godawari Manar	8.06	7.11	4.64	5.98	9.17	9.64	2.73	5.13	5.77	5.23	6
11.	Jai Jawan	7.72	7.41	8.03	5.48	10.84	9.32	7.61	8.48	10.17	12.19	9
12.	Manjra	12.03	13.19	14.96	12.08	15.59	10.15	8.04	9.22	10.33	11.40	12
13.	Tuljabhawani	6.34	5.54	4.17	1.23	3.53	3.10	2.57	2.50	4.04	4.44	4
14.	Terna	6.85	5.76	3.28	2.08	3.95	3.90	3.13	3.93	4.45	2.67	4
	Industry Average	8.68	7.58	5.64	4.27	7.93	6.49	3.78	5.07	5.8	6.17	6

Source: Annual reports of co-operative sugar factories under study from 1991-92 to 2000-2001.

also observed in 1993-94, reflecting decrease in sales with no significant change in receivables. It is clear that the factory has successed in controlling the receivables. Thereafter it showed fluctuation in receivables. The ratio was observed lower in remaining years of the study period.

In Parbhani district, the average receivables turnover ratio observed in Godawari Dudhana was 4 times, which is significantly lower than the average of Marathwada region, denoting the factory was not able to control over receivables. Highest ratio recorded was 9.41 times in 1991-92. Thereafter it showed decreasing trend for next 4 years of the study period. The lowest ratio ascertained was 0.65, expressing decrease in sales and increase in receivables. It shows unsatisfactory performance of receivables.

The average receivables turnover ratio in Purna observed was 5 times, which is lower than the average of Marathwada region. It showed much fluctuation in the ratio throughout the study period. The lowest ratio appeared was 3.25 times in 1991-92, reflecting decrease in sales. It showed very weak performance of receivables. Highest ratio recorded was 6.61 times in 1995-96, due to decrease in receivables. It indicates efficient control of the factory over receivables. This reveals efficient collection policy of factory in that year. The ratio was found less than 4 times in two years of the study period. It indicates poor control over receivables.

In Nanded district, the average receivables turnover ratio in Shankar observed was 5 times, which is lower than the average of Marathwada region, denoting inefficient control over receivables. The lowest ratio appeared was 2.83 times in 2000-01, reflecting increase in receivables. It showed unsatisfactory performance of receivables. This reveals that inefficient administration results in lower turnover of receivables. For profitability, a high turnover of receivables is necessary. The highest ratio shown was 6.63 in 1996-97, due to lower amount of receivables. It means, the receivables were under control in that year. The receivables turnover ratio observed was less than 5 times in five years of the study period. It indicates efficient collection policy.

The average receivables turnover ratio observed in Godawari Manar was 6 times, which is at par with the average of Marathwada region. It shows good control over receivables in 1991-92 and 1995-96, denoting lower amount of receivables. The highest ratio appeared was 9.64 in 1995-96 reflecting increase in sales and increase in receivables.

In Latur district the average receivables turnover ratio in Jai Jawan Jai Kisan was 9 times, showing efficient receivables management. It indicates good collection policy of receivables. The lowest ratio ascertained was 5.48, reflecting decrease in sales and increase in receivables. The highest ratio enlisted was 12.32 times in 2000-01, reflecting increase in sales. It indicates the ability of the factory in meeting the short-term obligations.

The average receivables turnover ratio in Manjra was 12 times, which was significantly higher than the average of Marathwada region. Manjra showed highest receivables turnover ratio among all fourteen factories studied. It indicates good performance of receivables among all factories studied. The lowest ratio observed was 8.04 times due to increase in receivables. The highest ratio recorded was 15.59 times in 1995-96, expressing good control over receivables. It shows that the factory has succeeded in controlling the receivables and recovered it in time. Hence, its short-term liquidity position seems to be satisfactory.

In Osmanabad district the average receivables turnover ratio observed in Tuljabhavani was 4 times, which was considerably lower than the average of Marathwada region. The factory showed satisfactory receivables turnover ratio in 1991-92 and 1992-93. Thereafter it showed fluctuating trend throughout the study period. The lowest ratio ascertained was 1.23 times in 1993-94, reflecting decrease in sales and increase in receivables. It was observed that the sale of sugar had decreased but receivables were not proportionately decreased. It indicates poor control over the receivables. The highest ratio appeared was 6.34 times in 1991-92. It was also observed that the receivables turnover ratio dropped below 6 times in 9 years of the study period. It is clears that the factory had failed in efficient control of its receivables.

In Terna, the average receivables turnover ratio observed was 4 times, expressing the inefficiency in receivables management. The average ratio is significantly lower than the average of Marathwada. The lowest ratio ascertained was 2.08 times in 1994-95, denoting decrease in sales and increase in receivables. It showed very weak performance of receivables. It is observed that only in two years of the study period the factory showed the ratio above 5 times.

It can be seen from Table 6.2 that there were ups and downs in the ratio over the years throughout the study period. The lowest ratio observed was 4 times in Sant Eknath, Godawari Dudhana, Tuljabhavani and Terna during the study period. The highest ratio observed was 12 times in Manjra. It indicates good control over receivables and better performance in receivables management.

In most of the sugar factories, the better position of receivables management is seen in the said table, because the receivables in sugar factories are not that much risky as credit sales in open account. Receivables in co-operative sugar factories comprises loans and advances which are given only after verifications of security of its recovery.

Fig. 6 (a) shows effective receivable turnover ratio in co-operative sugar factories studied.

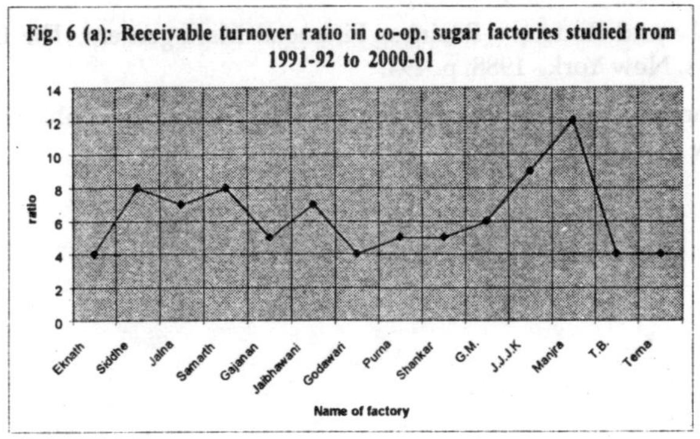

Control Over Receivables

The nature of receivables in co-operative sugar factories is different and control over receivables is also made by different manner. Control over receivables implies maintenance of receivables at an optimum level and to avoid excess and inadequate investment as to maximise the return. As discussed earlier, risk in receivables in sugar factories is less than risk in open account credit sales. For every component of receivables, in sugar factories, sufficient security is taken. The nature of receivables is loans and advances and these advances are recovered from the bills payable to concerned party. All receivables are against the payments to make in future, and thus control of recovery is easily possible in co-operative sugar factories.

There is no question about the inadequate investment in receivables as customers are not to be attracted through this investment. It is observed in the sugar factories studied that sufficient advances are paid to attract the contractors. It is also observed that no excess amount in loans and advances is invested which resulted into excess investment in receivables. It is also found that there are certain problems of control over loans and advances to harvesting and transportation contractors.

REFERENCES

1. S.C. Baradia, —Working Capital Management, Pointer Publishers, Jaipur, 1988, p. 113.
2. Weston and Brigham, —Essentials of Managerial Finance, The Dryden Press, Japan, 1985, p. 213.
3. Cooly and Roden, —Business Financial Management, The Dryden Press, New York, 1988, p. 494.
4. Ramesh K.S. Rao, —Financial Management, Macmillan Publishing Co., New York, 1987, p. 558.

7

Cash Management

Introduction

Cash is most important component of working capital. Cash is a basic input required to keep the firm running on continuous basis. Cash management is a core part of working capital management. Management of cash is essential to maintain sufficient cash required to business transactions and to avoid cash shortage. Excess cash should be invested in a profitable manner, but it should be available in time when it is needed.

Cash occupies an important position in the structure of working capital. A careful analysis of cash and its management is must. In this Chapter the concept of cash management is analysed by discussing certain important considerations like definition of cash, objective of holding cash, concept of cash management and functions of cash management.

From the discussion on the concept of cash, it is obvious that the term cash is used in two senses, narrow and broad. In narrow sense, cash means cash in hand and at Bank. But in broad sense cash means, cash in hand and at Bank, currency, cheques, bank drafts and deposits to be drawn at very short notice.

For cash management purposes, however, cash is used broadly to cover cash and generally accepted equivalent of cash such as deposits in bank, cheques in hand and in transit, bank drafts, money order and also marketable securities, which are short-term investments, excluding fixed deposits.

According to A.E. Reed, "Now a days non-availability and high cost of money have created a serious problem for industry. Nevertheless, cash, like any other assets of a company, is treated as a tool for profits. By its nature cash is an asset which is the least productive in itself and holding it inactive gives rise to a cost which may be termed as opportunity cost. This cost is equal to the profits that could have been earned, had the cash been put to some use. If a company is able to earn, say 15 per cent on the investment of funds internally, this will be the cost of holding cash inactive. This cash consciousness of enterprises had led to a change in the traditional role of cash management. Today the emphasis is on the right amount of cash, at the right time, at the right place, and at right cost."[1]

Objective of Holding Cash

Companies hold cash because the timing and amount of cash inflows do not match the timing and amount of cash outflows. Generally following are the objectives of holding cash:

(i) To meet the liquidity for routine outflows of the business;

(ii) To provide the liquidity for routine outflows;

(iii) To provide cash to scheduled major outlays;

(iv) To provide liquidity to unexpected drains;

(v) To meet bank relationship.

Cash in the business may be compared to the blood of the human body. Blood gives life and strength to human body and cash imparts life and strength, i.e. profit and solvency to organisation[2]. As the continuous generation and circulation of blood is necessary for the health of the human body, cash also must be continuously generated and circulated in the business for its health. This suggests for management of cash.

All this discussion lead to the core area of cash management that is maintaining the sound liquidity, minimising cost of holding cash and maximising return on investment of excess cash.

Cash management is concerned with minimising unproductive cash balances, investing temporarily excess cash advantageously and to making best possible arrangements for meeting planned and unexpected demands on the firm's cash[3].

Nature and Components of Cash in Co-operative Sugar Factories

Cash occupies an important position in the structure of working capital. It is the beginning as well as the end of operating cycle of a manufacturing concern. Cash management is concerned with minimising unproductive cash balances, investing temporary cash and making the best possible arrangements for meeting planned and unexpected demands on the firm's cash.

In co-operative sugar factories the term cash is used as cash in hand, cash at bank in all bank accounts (including current accounts and saving accounts) and some near cash items like stamps, bonds, postal deposits, etc. Items other than cash in hand and cash at bank are very rarely found in the balance sheets of co-operative sugar factories studied. It is also found that there is no investment in marketable securities made by sugar factories studied. The surplus cash is used either to reduce the loan balances or capital investment purpose. So cash management in co-operative sugar factories refers to only management of cash inflows and cash outflows and not marketable securities management. The concept of cash is taken for management as cash in hand and cash at bank in all bank accounts, including current accounts and saving accounts. Cash in hand and cash at bank are components of cash in co-operative sugar factories.

Cash Inflows

Cash comes in to co-operative sugar factories by different ways, which are discussed as follows:

(i) Sale of Sugar

The main and important source of cash inflow in sugar factories is sale of sugar. Sugar is sold as per Government Policy.

Government purchases levy sugar quota at levy price determined by it. The price determination is based generally on costs of production. Sugar is sold as per the 'release quota mechanism' of Central Government. Government fixes the quota of sugar to be released in a particular month by every sugar factory. The release orders are issued to sugar factories tri-monthly and factories have to sell the sugar accordingly. Levy sugar is purchased by government through district supply officer from the factories of that particular district. Free sugar is sold in open market by inviting tenders. It should be noted that both the sales are cash sales. No credit sales are permitted in co-operative sugar factories. Though this is the main source of cash, it is adjusted against working capital loan. Cash from sales of sugar is not directly received by co-operative sugar factories and cannot be directly used.

(ii) Sale of by-products

Sale of by-products is another important source of cash. The main by-products are molasses, bagasse and press mud. All these by-products are used for various purposes, as they got demand in market. Molasses is a major by-product, which gives substantial income to sugar factories. Bagasse and press mud have not much value in view of income.

(iii) Deposits

The third source of cash inflow in co-operative sugar factories is deposits from farmers. Two types of deposits are raised by co-operative sugar factories—Refundable deposits and non-refundable deposits. Refundable deposits are used for working capital purpose and non-refundable deposits are used for capital expenditure purpose. Some efficiently managed factories rely for working capital upon refundable deposits. Farmers also give good response to refundable deposits.

(iv) Working Capital Loans

In all co-operative sugar factories, working capital is raised through working capital loans from co-operative banks. Maharashtra State Co-operative Bank is the main agency disbursing working capital loans to co-operative sugar factories on the guarantee of State Government. Two types of loans are given to sugar factories 'Pre-seasonal Finance' and 'Seasonal Finance'. Pre-seasonal finance is given for the pre-seasonal expenses like administrative expenses, repairs and maintenance of plant and machinery, advances to harvesting and transport contractors, advances to farmers for cultivating cane and for other miscellaneous purposes. Seasonal finance is given for meeting the production and administration cost of crushing season. Both finance are against stock of sugar and stock of stores and spares.

(v) Capital Source

The other source of cash may be issue of share capital and long-term loans. But as these are used mostly for capital expenditure like plant, machinery, buildings, etc., they may not be regarded as cash source for working capital.

(vii) Operative Profit

The cash comes through sales and sales include the portion of profit, which is an additional source of cash. The working capital increases by amount of profit. Thus profit may be the source of working capital. For cash source purpose, net profit concept can not be used as source of cash. The term profit is taken as 'cash profit' or operative profit.

From the above analysis it can be concluded that the sale of by-products, working capital loan and refundable short-term deposits are the major cash inflows in co-operative sugar factories.

Cash Outflows

The major cash outflows in co-operative sugar factories are discussed as under:

(i) Payment to Farmers Against Purchase of Cane

The major cash outflow is the payment to farmers for cane purchases. Major part of working capital loan is used to pay the cane price. Special arrangements are made by government to protect the interest of farmers. The farmer's payment for cane purchases is made through a special bank account. Withdrawals from this account are allowed only for cane payment. This is the major utilisation of working capital.

(ii) Payment of Harvesting and Transport Expenses

Payment of harvesting and transportation expenses is second major cash outflow. These expenses are also paid, out of working capital loans. Some advance are paid before commencement of crushing season and final payment is made at the end of the crushing season with recovery of advances.

(iii) Repairs and Maintenance Expenses

Repairs and maintenance of plant and machinery is peculiar feature of co-operative sugar factory. The product and production process is such that repairs and maintenance before commencement of crushing season are necessary. Contract for repairs and maintenance is given to engineering firms. Some advance is paid and final payment is made with recovery of advance.

(iv) Purchase of Stores and Spares

Another major cash outflow is for purchase of stores and spares. This includes chemicals, gunny bags and other consumable stores. Tenders are invited and stores are purchased as per the regulations of the Commissioner—sugar, Pune.

(v) Loans to Farmers

For sugarcane development and agricultural development, loans are paid to member farmers by co-operative sugar factories. For this, funds are received from Central Government. Sugar factory works as an agency for finance and recovery of such loans. Though this is part of cash outflow, it is made out of funds received for this purpose.

(vi) Refund of Deposit

Some deposits are refunded after their maturity, with interest. Generally deposits are collected through cane bills and refunded on their maturity.

(vii) Refund of Working Capital Loans and Interest

Payment of working capital loans with interest is made through sales of sugar. Sales proceeds of sugar are directly deposited in working capital loan account.

(viii) Administration Expenses

This payment is recurring payment in the form of salaries, office expenses, legal expenses, insurance, interest, deposits for customs and excise, etc.

(ix) Capital Payment

The cash outflows for capital payments may be for purchase of plant, machinery, land, building, refund of government capital, refund of long-term loan, etc. These payments are made out of sale of sugar. But other sources like non-refundable deposits, members share capital are also used for such payments, as sales of sugar are first adjusted with working capital loan.

It can be known from the above discussion that sources for working capital are strictly used to finance the current assets. Other disbursements are made out of capital sources or long-term sources. The financial structure of co-operative sugar factory is regulated by government and financial institutions in such a way that not much is left in the hands of management of these factories.

Growth of Cash

Table 7.1 shows the growth in cash balances held by co-operative sugar factories during the study period. The growth is shown by growth percentage based on the base year 1991-92.

In Aurangabad district, the growth percentage of Sant Eknath shows a range between 30% to 1746%. It showed higher growth percentage in 1999-2000 and 2000-01, as the size of cash was high. This reveals that the cash position was better in the last two years of the study period than remaining years. The growth index of Siddheshwar moved between 20% to 115% during the same period. It showed upward and downward trend. Cash index is less than 100 in eight years of the study period. This reveals that the cash trends are on the decline in almost nine years.

Jalna showed lower growth percentage throughout the study period as the size of base year's cash was high. It showed growth index less than 100 in all years of the study period. It means cash balance had decreased betwèen 1991-92 and 2000-01. Samarth showed continuous growth percentage of cash except 1996-97.

Growth percentage ranges from 100% to 874% during the period of study. Samarth showed better cash position as growth index showed increasing trends.

In Beed district, Gajanan showed ups and downs every year. The growth percentage moved from 45% to 546%, with an average growth percentage of 169%. Jaibhavani showed the growth percentage of cash in the range of 100% to 832% with an average growth percentage of 322%. This reveals good cash position of the factory. Godawari Dhudhana recorded ups and downs in growth index. The percentage of growth is shown between 43% to 534%, with an average of 176%. Purna also recorded ups and downs in the growth of cash. The growth index moved from 43% to 322%, with an average of 176%. It showed growth index on the decline up to zero in the year 1997-98. The cash balance was very less in that year. This shows very poor cash position of the factoy.

In Nanded district, the average growth in size of cash recorded by Shankar was 185% with the range from 29% to 376%. Godawari Manar showed a relatively higher growth. Jai Jawan Jai Kisan recorded a growth between 18% and 337%. It showed ups and downs every year during the study period. Manjra recorded ups and downs in growth index. It ranges from 34% to 177% with an average of 96%. It showed growth index less than 100 for 5 years of the study period. It means cash position of the factory was not so good because sale proceeds of sugar were used for specified purpose which resulted in lower cash balance. The growth percentage moved from 100% to 507% with an average growth percentage of 269% in Tuljabhavani. The growth index of Terna moved between100% and 1095% and the average growth index shown by Terna was 529%. The factory has shown growth index more than 100 in total ten years of the study period. This reveals good cash position of the factory.

It can be seen from Table 7.1 that on an average the growth index of size of cash in the sugar factories studied moved between 52% and 529%. The lowest is of Jalna and highest is of Terna. Highest average size of cash is also shown by Terna and lowest by Gajanan. This reveals that there had been huge fluctuations in the sizes and growth rates of cash in sugar factories studied.

Table—7.1: Growth Indices of Cash in Co-operative Sugar Factories Under Study

Sl.No.	Name of the Factory	91-92	92-93	93-94	94-95	95-96	96-97	97-98	98-99	99-00	00-01	Average
01.	Sant Eknath	100	189	78	120	152	209	30	207	1746	1474	431
02.	Siddheshwar	100	89	96	60	52	44	20	70	115	92	74
03.	Jalna	100	56	54	10	38	43	53	58	94	13	52
04.	Samarth	100	171	178	194	236	111	193	481	236	874	277
05.	Gajanan	100	97	51	296	282	45	47	102	546	127	169
06.	Jaibhavani	100	832	131	287	125	153	429	331	597	237	322
07.	Godawari Dudhana	100	80	359	534	294	50	112	56	43	132	176
08.	Purna	100	102	81	292	208	43	0	101	282	322	153
09.	Shankar	100	295	376	103	48	29	313	418	84	86	185
10.	Godawari Manar	100	1543	6	34	178	60	31	187	17	0	216
11.	Jai Jawan	100	36	91	321	51	18	219	337	257	141	157
12.	Manjra	100	55	68	34	47	156	54	130	136	177	96
13.	Tuljabhavani	100	233	202	234	394	293	241	260	507	222	269
14.	Terna	100	341	215	214	859	224	921	466	851	1095	529

Source: Annual reports of co-operative sugar factories under study from 1991-92 to 2000-2001.

Sugar factories need sufficient liquid sources in order to meet its day to day expenses and cane bills. Better liquidity support ensures smooth working. The cash position shows neither increasing nor decreasing trend. Hence, minimum required amount of cash should be made available, avoiding liquidity problems in short run.

Control Over Cash

One of the major objectives of cash management from the standpoint of increasing return on investment is to economise on the cash holdings without impairing the overall liquidity requirement of the firm. This is possible by effecting higher control over cash flow[4].

The following important ratios indicate the achievement of the firm in this regard:

(i) Cash to sales ratio;

(ii) Cash to working capital ratio.

(i) Cash to Sales Ratio

This is one of the important ratios of controlling cash. A study of cash to sales ratio will provide a deep insight into the cash balances held by the concerns. To examine the efficiency of cash management, it is meaningful to know the cash to sales ratio. The cash to sales ratio in co-operative sugar factories for the period of study from 1991-92 to 2000-01 has been presented in Table 7.2. Cash to sales ratio is calculated by using the following formula:

$$\text{Cash to sales ratio} = \frac{\text{Cash}}{\text{Sales}} \times 100$$

A lower cash to sales ratio indicates a poor liquid position of the factory, while higher cash to sales ratio indicates a sound liquid position of the factory.

Factory-wise Cash to Sales Ratio

The industry average of cash to sales ratio in the co-operative sugar factories studied in Marathwada region for the study period, i.e. from 1991-92 to 2000-01, ascertained was 4 per cent.

In Aurangabad district, Sant Eknath registered a fluctutating trend during the period of study. It was 1 per cent in 1991-92, which increased to 9 per cent in 1999-2000. The average cash to sales ratio observed was 3 per cent which was less than the average of the Marathwada region. The factory showed highest ratio of 9% in the year 1999-2000 due to huge amount of cash. In this year factory showed good liquidity position. The average cash to sales ratio of Siddheshwar was 3 per cent. The lowest cash to sales ratio appeared was 1% in 1997-98, due to small amount of cash and highest ratio recorded was 7 per cent in 1993-94 due to considerably lower sales.

In Jalna district, the average cash to sales ratio in Jalna for the given period of ten years was 4 per cent, which was equal to the average of Marathwada region. The lowest ratio ascertained was 1 per cent in 1994-95, due to little cash balance, while highest ratio observed was 16 per cent in 1997-98. The ratio was found more in this year due to little sales volume. The cash balance do not make any difference but it showed very small amount of sale of sugar. Hence, the ratio observed was higher in that year, still liquidity position of the factory found very weak. The average cash to sales ratio of Samarth was 4 per cent. The lowest ratio appeared was 1 per cent in 1996-97, due to little amount of cash in comparison to other years of the study period.

In Beed district, the average cash to sales ratio in Gajanan was 5 per cent for the given study period of ten years. Highest ratio appeared was 18 per cent in 1994-95, due to little sales and higher amount of cash. The lowest ratio ascertained was 1 per cent in 1991-92 and 1996-97 due to little amount of cash. The average cash to sales ratio of Jai Bhavani was 5 per cent. Lowest ratio was recorded 1 per cent in 1991-92, 1995-96 and 2000-01, due to very poor amount of cash. The highest ratio registered was 13 per cent in 1992-93 and 1994-95. The ratio was found higher due to more amount of cash. The lower cash to sales ratio indicates the poor liquid position of the factory, while higher cash to sales ratio indicates the good liquidity position.

Table—7.2: Cash to Sales Ratio in Co-operative Sugar Factories Under Study

Sl.No.	Name of the Factory	91-92	92-93	93-94	94-95	95-96	96-97	97-98	98-99	99-00	00-01	Average
01.	Sant Eknath	1	2	1	3	2	2	1	2	9	5	3
02.	Siddeshwar	4	4	7	3	2	2	1	3	3	2	3
03.	Jalna SSK	4	3	2	1	2	2	16	5	4	1	4
04.	Samarth	2	4	5	8	4	1	4	5	2	5	4
05.	Gajanan	1	4	8	18	4	1	3	2	7	1	5
06.	Jai Bhavani	1	13	5	13	1	2	7	3	5	1	5
07.	Godawari Dudhna	1	1	6	21	4	1	3	3	1	2	4
08.	Purna	3	3	2	8	4	1	0	2	6	5	3
09.	Shankar	3	8	13	4	1	1	9	11	2	2	5
10.	Godawari Manar	1	9	0	0	1	0	0	1	0	0	1
11.	Jai Jawan	2	1	2	9	1	0	3	4	3	1	3
12.	Manjra	3	2	2	1	1	3	1	2	2	2	2
13.	Tuljabhavani	3	7	7	21	10	8	7	7	9	4	8
14.	Terna	2	8	8	8	11	3	11	4	5	6	6
	Industry Average	3	5	5	7	3	2	5	4	4	3	4

Source: Annual reports of co-operative sugar factories under study from 1991-92 to 2000-2001.

In Parbhani district, the average cash to sales ratio in Godawari Dudhana was 4 per cent, which was equal to the average of Marathwada. It showed fluctuating trends during the period of study. The lowest ratio recorded was 1 per cent in 1991-92, 1992-93, 1996-97 and 1999-2000 due to very little amount of cash. It shows poor liquidity position of the factory. The highest ratio ascertained was 21 per cent in 1994-95 due to very little sales volume in this year.

The average cash to sales ratio of Purna in the study period of ten years was 3 per cent, which was less than the average of Marathwada region. The lowest ratio appeared was less than one per cent in 1999-2000, due to very negligible amount of cash. The highest ratio ascertained was 8 per cent in 1994-95. The ratio observed was high due to more amounts of cash and little sales volume. It shows better liquidity position of the factory. The ratio was found less than 3 per cent in four years. This indicates weak liquid position of the factory.

In Nanded district, the average cash to sales ratio of Shankar was 5 per cent, which was more than the average of the Marathwada region. It is an indication of sound liquid position of the factory. The highest ratio ascertained was 11 per cent in 1998-99 denoting higher amounts of cash and small amount of sales. It is also observed that the ratio was 9 per cent in 1997-98. This shows good cash position of the factory.

The average cash to sales ratio of Godawari Manar was 1 per cent, which was extremely lower than the standard. It indicates a very poor cash position of the factory. The lowest ratio observed was less than 1 per cent in five years of the study period, due to very negligible amount of cash. The ratio was found one per cent in three years of the study period. The highest ratio appeared was 9 per cent in only one year, i.e. 1992-93, due to higher amount of cash.

In Latur district, the average cash to sales ratio of Jai Jawan Jai Kisan was 3 per cent. The lowest ratio observed was less than one per cent in 1996-97, due to little amount of cash. It indicates poor liquid position of the factory. The highest ratio recorded was 9 per cent in 1994-95 due to higher amount of cash and lower sales volume. Higher ratio indicates better liquidity position of the factory. During the entire period, except 1994-95, the ratio observed was below 4 per cent, which indicates feeble cash position of the factory.

The average cash to sales ratio of Manjra observed was 2 per cent. It indicates weak liquidity position of the factory. The lowest ratio appeared was 1 per cent in 1994-95, 1995-96 and 1997-98 due to little amount of cash. The highest ratio of 3 per cent was recorded in 1991-92 and 1996-97, due to lower sales volume. During the entire study period, the ratio had been below 3 per cent, which indicates poor liquidity position of the factory.

In Osmanabad district, the average cash to sales ratio of Tuljabhavani was 8 per cent, which indicates sound liquidity position of the factory. The highest ratio recorded was 21 per cent in 1994-95, due to lower sales volume. The lowest ratio ascertained was 3 per cent in 1991-92, due to little amount of cash. It is observed that, this factory showed good liquid position among the all factories studied. It can be observed from the above analysis that the ratio in Tuljabhavani was higher as compared to remaining factories under study. Though this indicates sound liquidity position, but at the same time, it also shows that a significant position of cash balances had been remained unused, which the factory could have otherwise profitably used.

The average cash to sales ratio in Terna was observed 6 per cent, which is more than the average of Marathwada region. It is the indication of sound liquidity position of the factory. The lowest ratio recorded was 2 per cent in 1991-92, due to little amount of cash. The highest ratio observed was 11 per cent in 1995-96 and 1997-98. It indicates the significant cash position of the factory.

It reveals from the Table 7.2 that average cash to sale ratio is more in Tuljabhavani and less in Godawari Manar. High ratio indicates better liquidity and sound cash position of the factory, while lower ratio indicates poor cash position of the factory. Therefore, it may be recommended that, factory should concentrate on strengthening the cash position to avoid the weakness of the factory.

It should be noted that sales of sugar and by-products are made in cash in sugar factories and the amount thus accrued is directly deposited in loan account and not in bank accounts. This may be the reason for lower cash balance.

(ii) Cash to Working Capital Ratio

Cash is an important component of working capital. It is the duty of the financial manager to maintain a sound liquidity position of the firm so that obligations may be settled well in time. If the firm maintains a small cash balance, its liquidity becomes weak and suffers from paucity of cash to make payments.

Cash to working capital ratio is one of the important ratios of controlling cash. A study of cash to working capital ratio will provide a deep insight into the cash balances held in the business. To examine the efficiency of cash management, it is meaningful to know the cash to working capital ratio. Table 7.3 gives information about the cash to working capital ratio in co-operative sugar factories studied for the period from 1991-92 to 2000-01.

To calculate the ratio of cash to working capital, following formula is used.

$$\text{Cash to working capital} = \frac{\text{Cash and Bank}}{\text{Working capital}} \times 100$$

This ratio is meaningful and correct measurement of liquidity. It provides a clear picture of firm's stability of cash position.

Factory-wise Cash to Working Capital Ratio

In Aurangabad district, the average cash to working capital ratio of Sant Eknath was 2 per cent. The average ratio for all factories studied in Marathwada region was found to be 3 per cent. Sant Eknath showed this ratio less than the average of Marathwada region. Lowest ratio observed was 1 per cent in five years of the study period, due to small amount of cash. The highest ratio recorded was 8 per cent in 1999-2000, due to higher amount of cash.

The average cash to working capital ratio of Siddeshwar was 3 per cent, which was as per with the average of Marathwada. The lowest ratio ascertained was 1 per cent in 1996-97, due to little amount of cash. The highest ratio appeared was 7 per cent in 1992-93, stating higher amount of cash. It was an indication of sound cash position of the factory. Lower ratio is an indication of poor cash position of the factory.

In Jalna district, the average cash to working capital ratio of Jalna was 4 per cent. It was considerably higher than the average of Marathwada. The lowest ratio observed was less than one per cent in 1994-95 and 2000-01, due to very negligible cash balance. It results in poor liquid position. The ratio was observed almost zero per cent in two years, i.e. 1994-95 and 2000-01, due to huge stock of sugar blocking heavy amount of cash.

The average cash to working capital ratio of Samarth was 4 per cent. It was also higher than the average of Marathwada. It may be observed that factory has been successful in maintaining sound cash position. Hence, its short-term financial position seems to be satisfactory. The lowest ratio ascertained was 1 per cent in 1996-97 due to little amount of cash. All remaining years of the study period showed good liquidity position.

In Beed district, the average cash to working capital ratio of Gajanan observed was 3 per cent, which is the same as the average of Marathwada. Lowest ratio appeared was 1 per cent in 1996-97, 1998-99 and 2000-01, due to little amount of cash. The highest ratio observed was 6 per cent in 1995-96. It indicates better cash position of the factory. The ratio was found less than 2 per cent in five years of the study period. It was revealed that a very low amount of cash balances were kept by the factory. Hence, its cash position seems to be unsatisfactory.

The average cash to working capital ratio of Jaibhavani is 4 per cent, which is higher than the average of Marathwada. It may be observed that the factory has maintained sufficient cash balance to meet its financial needs. It shows good liquidity position of the factory. The lowest ratio ascertained was 1 per cent in 1996-97, due to small amount of cash. The highest ratio observed was 17 per cent, due to higher cash balance and lower current assets.

Table—7.3: Cash to Working Capital Ratio in Co-operative Sugar Factories Under Study

Sl.No.	*Name of the Factory*	*91-92*	*92-93*	*93-94*	*94-95*	*95-96*	*96-97*	*97-98*	*98-99*	*99-00*	*00-01*	*Average*
01.	Sant Eknath	1%	2%	2%	1%	1%	2%	1%	1%	8%	4%	2%
02.	Siddheshwar	6%	7%	5%	2%	2%	1%	2%	2%	3%	2%	3%
03.	Jalna	6%	3%	3%	–	2%	6%	12%	3%	4%	-	4%
04.	Samarth	3%	5%	7%	3%	2%	1%	3%	5%	2%	5%	4%
05.	Gajanan	2%	5%	3%	5%	6%	1%	2%	1%	5%	1%	3%
06.	Jaibhawani	2%	17%	5%	3%	2%	1%	5%	2%	3%	1%	4%
07.	Godawari	1%	1%	6%	4%	2%	–	2%	1%	1%	1%	2%
08.	Purna	2%	2%	2%	5%	4%	1%	–	2%	4%	3%	3%
09.	Shankar	4%	11%	11%	2%	1%	1%	8%	8%	1%	1%	5%
10.	Godawari Manar	1%	10%	–	–	1%	–	–	1%	–	2%	1%
11.	Jai Jawan	2%	1%	2%	5%	1%	–	3%	3%	2%	1%	2%
12.	Manjra	5%	2%	3%	1%	1%	3%	1%	2%	2%	2%	2%
13.	Tuljabhawani	3%	7%	12%	6%	8%	5%	4%	5%	7%	3%	6%
14.	Terna	2%	9%	7%	2%	8%	21%	7%	4%	4%	3%	5%
	Industry Average	3%	6%	5%	3%	3%	2%	2%	3%	3%	2%	3%

Source: Annual reports of co-operative sugar factories under study from 1991-92 to 2000-2001.

In Parbhani district, the Godawari Dudhana showed average cash to working capital ratio at 2 per cent, which is less than the average of Marathwada region. The lowest ratio was appeared almost less than 1 per cent in 1996-97, denoting very negligible cash balance. The cash position was negligible because of huge stock of inventory blocking heavy amount. It reveals poor liquidity position of the factory. The highest ratio observed was 6 per cent in 1993-94, due to limited working capital. It does not show good liquidity.

The average cash to working capital ratio of Purna is 3 per cent, which is equal to the average of Marathwada. The lowest ratio found was less than one per cent in 1997-98, due to very little amount of cash. Highest ratio observed was 5 per cent in 1994-95. It shows good liquid position of the factory. Purna shows higher cash in 2000-01, till ratio is lower, due to higher amount of working capital, i.e. inventory and receivables. The ratio is found below 2 per cent in 7 years of the study period, creating a challenge before factory.

In Nanded district, the average cash to working capital ratio of Shankar is 5 per cent, which is significantly higher than the average of Marathwada. It intimates good cash position of the factory. The lowest ratio ascertained 1 per cent in 1995-96, 1996-97 and 2000-01, expressing unsatisfactory cash position of the factory. Highest ratio appeared was 11 per cent in 1992-93 and 1993-94, due to higher amount of cash. The ratio observed above 8 per cent in four years. It indicates sound liquid position of the factory.

The average cash to working capital ratio of Godawari Manar is 1 per cent, stating inadequate cash position. It results in inability of the factory in meeting the day-to-day obligations. It will be great obstacle in making the payments of outstanding dues. The highest ratio observed was 10 per cent in 1992-93, due to high amount of cash. It showed a good liquid position of the factory. The lowest ratio ascertained was less than one per cent in almost five years of the study period, due to very little amount of cash. The cash is observed very negligible because the factory has maintained huge stock of sugar and thus it affects the cash position of the factory.

In Latur district, the average cash to working capital ratio of Jai Jawan Jai Kisan is 2 per cent, stating weak position of cash. The highest ratio recorded was 5 per cent in 1994-95, expressing satisfactory cash position. Lowest ratio was appeared less than one per cent in 1996-97. It also observed that the ratio below 2 per cent in four years of the study period, which indicates feeble cash position of the factory.

The average cash to working capital ratio of Manjra was observed 2 per cent, which is less than the average of Marathwada region. The highest ratio ascertained was 5 per cent in 1991-92 due to high amount of cash. The highest cash amount was found in 2000-01, still ratio 2 per cent, because of higher amount of working capital. The cash is observed lower in relation to working capital. The lowest ratio ascertained was 1 per cent in 1994-95, 1995-96 and 1997-98, expressing poor liquid position of the factory.

In Osmanabad district, the average cash to working capital ratio of Tuljabhavani observed is 6 per cent, which is considerably higher than the average of Marathwada region. It showed sound liquid position of the factory. The lowest ratio ascertained was 3 per cent in 1991-92 and 2000-01, expressing weak cash position of the factory. The highest ratio observed was 12 per cent in 1993-94, stating better liquid position. It may be observed that the ratio is above 4 per cent in 8 years of the study period.

The average cash to working capital ratio of Terna was observed 5 per cent, which is higher than the average of Marathwada region. It showed good cash position of the factory. It may be observed that the factory has succeeded in maintaining good liquidity position. Hence, its cash positions seems to be satisfactory. The lowest ratio appeared was 2 per cent in 1991-92, 1994-95 and 1996-97, due to little amount of cash. It showed weak liquid position of the factory. The highest ratio ascertained was 9 per cent in 1992-93. The ratio was observed above 7 per cent in four years of the study period.

It may be observed from Table 7.3 that the average cash to working capital ratio is 3 per cent. The average ratio of Tuljabhavani found highest, i.e. 6 per cent among all factories studied, while lowest ratio is observed, 1 per cent in, Godawari

Manar. Higher ratio shows a good liquid position of the factory, but on other hand it also shows idle cash balances.

REFERENCES

1. A.E. Reed, —Corporate Cash Management, Financial Executive, London, Oct. 1963.
2. Kulkarni and Satyaprasad, —Financial Management, Hamalaya Publishing House, Delhi, 1999, p. 774.
3. Hunt and Williams as quoted by K. Rajeshwar Rao, —Working Capital Planning and Control in Public Enterprises in India, Ajantha Publication, New Delhi, 1985, p. 31.
4. N.K. Agrawal, —Management of Working Capital, Sterling Publishers, New Delhi, p. 38.

8

Summary, Conclusions and Suggestions

Sugar industry, in recent times, has acquired great significance in India. This industry is the second largest agro-based industry in India. Its contribution to the national wealth and employment generation cannot be set aside. The effective administration of working capital helps in understanding the survival and growth of sugar industry. The mode of management of working capital determines, to very large extent, the success or failure of overall operations of business. Proper management of working capital has become crucial and important for the success of business.

This chapter proposes to present summary and conclusions of the study and suggestions based on conclusions. Summary and conclusions are separately recorded for all aspects of working capital management, which were taken for study.

A. SUMMARY

1. Introduction

The Government of India appointed a committee under the Chairmanship of Shri Gorwala in 1951. This committee made recommendations to promote the co-operative processing societies of farmers and linking of agricultural credit with agricultural marketing. In 1956 Central Government adopted a preferential licensing policy for development of co-operative sugar factories, i.e. from second five-year plan onwards. Co-operative sugar industry in India progressed continuously and dominated the private sugar industry. The number of sugar factories in India increased from 140 in 1950-51 to 436 in 2000-01. The country has become self-sufficient in sugar production and started exporting sugar since second five-year plan.

The first sugar factory was established in Maharashtra in 1919 under the private sector. However, the real boost to sugar industry came with the setting up of first co-operative sugar factory at Loni in Ahmednagar district in 1950. In 1950-51 there was only one co-operative sugar factory in the state at Loni, and out of total 14 sugar factories 13 were in private sector. This has increased to 128 in 2000-01. The sugar production of Maharashtra increased from 1000 tons in 1960-61 to 6705 tons in 2000-01. The State of Maharashtra has maintained its leading position in co-operative sugar industry since its beginning. Maharashtra is the biggest sugar producer in co-operative sector in India. In Maharashtra, it is observed that, the sugar factories in private sector are gradually disappearing and co-operative sector has established 98% of sugar units in the state.

In Marathwada region the first sugar factory was established in 1957 in private sector. By the end of 1985, there were 22 co-operative sugar factories in Marathwada region. By the year 2000-01, the number went up to 36 sugar factories. The co-operative sugar sector has played a significant role in the economic development of rural Maharashtra and Marathwada region.

Though sugar industry has been delicensed since 1998, Central Government regulations are still in force.

In spite of the success of co-operative sugar industry in the state, it is facing various problems and has become a centre of criticisms. The sugar factories in the state are lagging behind in managerial efficiency. Many of the units (factories) are not able to control their cost of production and hence number of co-operative sugar factories in the state and particularly in the Marathwada region are carrying huge losses. The co-operative sugar factories in Marathwada has failed in solving its problems like inadequate supply of quality cane, increasing production cost, huge losses, low rate of sugar recovery, shortage of funds, etc. Working capital deficit is the common problem in all the co-operative sugar factories. Hence, proper management of working capital is very important for the success of the co-operative sugar factory.

The study of "management of working capital in sugar co-operatives" with special reference to Marathwada has undertaken with the same view. The main objective of the study is to examine the working capital management in co-operative sugar factories. Fourteen co-operative sugar factories were selected as sample units from Marathwada Region. The period of study was of ten years from 1991-92 to 2000-01. The study is presented in eight chapters, viz. Introduction, Review of Literature, Profile of the Sugar Factories included in the study, Working Capital Management—trends and liquidity analysis, Inventory Management, Receivable Management, Cash Management, and last, Summary, Conclusions and Suggestions.

Taking into account the importance of sugar industry in the national economy, number of researchers have worked on the various aspects of sugar industry, such as its growth, various problems of sugar industry and its prospects. Similarly, government policy and regional planning for sugar industry area, labour situation in the industry, impact of the industry on the lives of farmers and agriculture, financial management of sugar industry, importance of sugar co-operatives in rural economy and such other aspects of the industry have also been studied.

2. Working Capital Management—Trend and Liquidity Analysis

Working capital of a co-operative sugar factory is an amount required for the factory to manage the day to day activities of the business, e.g. buying of raw material, i.e. sugarcane. The crushing, of sugarcane continues for 6 months and above during the season. This period is called crushing season. When there is no crushing the period is called as 'off season'. Working capital in off-season is comparatively less than crushing season. In off-season working capital is required for repairs and maintenance of plant, purchase of stores and spares, gunny bags, payment of advance to harvesting and transportation contractors and administration expenses. In crushing season, working capital is required to purchase sugarcane, to pay harvesting and transportation expenses, payment to stores and spares and office and administrative expenses. Huge working capital funds are required in crushing season.

Working capital finance is made available to co-operative sugar factories through banks and various financial institutions. Government always gives strong financial support to co-operative sugar factories. Maharashtra State Co-operative Bank and district Central Co-operative Banks provide the finance to co-operative sugar factories to meet their working capital needs.

In co-operative sugar factories, excess investment is found in stock of sugar and spares. The working capital is excess in the form of current assets but cash becomes short. Deficit working capital position arises due to low speed of sales and low recovery of cash.

Working Capital Trends

Working capital trend analysis is important as it helps to judge the tendency of working capital and also helps to determine its efficiency. The working capital trend analysis is made by examining some important aspects like, current assets trend and current liabilities trend.

(i) Current Assets Trend

The size of gross working capital is continuously growing in all factories studied, during the study period of ten years from 1991-92 to 2000-01. The average annual size of gross working capital ranges from Rs. 1597 lakhs to Rs. 8151 lakhs among the factories studied.

It is observed in the study that the size of working capital in 2500 TCD factories like Siddheshwar, Samarth, Jaibhavani, Purna, Godawari Manar, Manjra and Terna are larger than remaining 1250 TCD factories. The reason is that, the production efficiency of 2500 TCD factories is more than 1250 TCD factories. Hence production of sugar is more in 2500 TCD factories which resulted into increase in the size of current assets. Such is not the case of 1250 TCD factories because of certain reasons. The main reason of low production efficiency is inadequate supply and low quality of sugarcane.

The structure of working capital in all sugar factories studied is same. The components of working capital are inventories, receivables and cash and bank balance. These components are indicated as current assets in the annual balance sheets of co-operative sugar factories.

Components analysis of working capital reveals that, inventory is the major component of current assets, which occupy 65% to 87% share in current assets in all sugar factories studied. All factories show same tendency. The reason, in all factories, is huge stock of sugar. The share of another component, receivables, is on an average 11% to 33%, and the share of third component, i.e. cash and bank, is not more than 1% to 6% in all sugar factories studied.

Working capital indices show the growing trend of investment in working capital. The average growth index ranges from 106% to 270% in the factories studied. The growth index is higher in 2500 TCD factories than 1250 TCD factories. This indicates a higher investment in current assets in 2500 TCD factories as compared to 1250 TCD factories.

(ii) Current Liabilities Trend

The size of current liabilities has been continuously growing in all factories during the study period. On an average, the size of current liabilities was between Rs. 1819 Lakhs and Rs. 7587 lakhs per year. It is observed that 2500 TCD factories like Samarth, Jaibhavani, Purna, Godawari Manar, Manjra and Terna (exception Siddheshwar) have large amounts of current liabilities than 1250 TCD factories. The reason behind this is large amount of working capital loans utilised by 2500 TCD factories.

While examining the share of components of current liabilities, it is found that the large share is occupied by the components of working capital loans and equally by creditors and outstanding expenses together. The share of working capital loan in current liability ranges from 40% to 55% in all factories. The share of other components, i.e. creditors and outstanding expenses, is between 45% and 60%. It is found that working capital loan is a permanent and major component of current liabilities in all sugar factories.

Trend of current liabilities is examined by using growth indices. The base year taken is 1991-92. The average growth index, in all factories, vary from 126% to 407%. It is found that the growth in the current liability is more in all sugar factories in general. It is increasing more in 2500 TCD factories. Though size of current liabilities is more in 2500 TCD in comparison to 1250 TCD factories, the tendency of growth indices is more or less the same in both the factory groups.

Efficiency of Working Capital

The efficiency of working capital management in co-operative sugar factories is discussed with the help of working capital turnover ratio.

Working Capital Turnover

The working capital turnover analysis indicates very poor performance of working capital management. Out of fourteen factories, only three factories showed the ratio more than 1 and remaining eleven factories showed less than 1. It reveals that the speed of sales in all factories is slow than expected. The reason behind low turnover is found that the sales are regulated by government and factories are not free to sell the sugar at their own. Another reason is that the State Government does not lift the levy sugar quota from factories in time, even though they put in their purchase orders. The quantities of levy sugar purchased by government are shown as stock till they are delivered to government and hence working capital turnover ratios are lower in all factories. The selling process of sugar is lengthy and working capital turnover ratio tends to be lower in sugar industry in comparison with other industries.

The average working capital turnover ratio of all fourteen co-operative sugar factories ranges from 0.63 to 1.10 during the study period of ten years. The average highest ratio observed was

1.10 in Siddheshwar and Manjra and lowest 0.63 in Godawari Dudhana. It is observed that the ratios are minimum in the year 1994-95 and maximum in 1991-92 in most of the sugar factories.

Liquidity Analysis

The objective of working capital management is to maintain liquidity of the firm. Liquidity analysis is a tool to assess the performance of working capital management. The liquidity position is analysed with the help of current ratio and quick ratio.

(i) Current Ratio

The ideal current ratio recommended is 2:1, but only Siddheshwar showed this ratio more than 2:1 in 1991-92 to 1993-94 and 1997-98. No other factory touched this figure during the study period. It is observed that the highest average current ratio 1.86:1 is shown by Siddheshwar and lowest average ratio 0.39 is shown by Gajanan during the study period of ten years. It reveals that liquidity position of Siddheshwar is better among all factories and very poor liquidity position of Gajanan. It is also observed that the highest average current ratio is 1:16 in 1991-92 and lowest 0.95 in 1996-97 during the study period of ten years.

(ii) Quick Ratio

The quick ratio or acid test ratio is important device to test the short-term financial strength of the business. It is an improved testing instrument of assessing liquidity position of the business than current ratio. The rule of thumb is 1:1 for the quick ratio. If a business has a quick ratio of at least 100%, it is considered to be a fairly good current financial position. A ratio less than one indicates a poor financial position of the factory.

The ideal quick ratio recommended is 1:1, but not a single sugar factory, among the factories studied, touched this level. It shows very poor liquidity position of the factories. It is observed that the sugar factories under study have been failed in equalizing the liquid assets with liquid liabilities. It is revealed from the quick ratio analysis that the short-term financial position of sugar factories under study was very poor.

It is observed that, the highest average quick ratio during the study period of 0.39:1 was shown by Siddheshwar and lowest of 0.11:1 by Godawari Manar.

3. Inventory Management

Inventory occupies a major share in the structure of working capital. Holding of inventories results into costs and benefits, so the management of inventories affects the profitability of the firm. Various factors like inventory costs, funds available, rate of consumption, lead-time, availability of required materials and management policy determine the size of inventories.

Inventory of a co-operative sugar factory comprises the stocks of work in progress, finished goods and stores and spares. It is observed in sugar factories that, on an average inventory occupies 65% to 87% shares in current assets. There is no raw material inventory in sugar factories.

Free sale of sugar is not allowed to sugar factories. All factories have to sell sugar under the control of government. Sales are made on the basis of monthly quota allotted to each factory. Government totally regulates the supply of sugar. Levy sale quota is purchased by State Government at a prescribed price determined by it. This quota of sugar is used by government to sell under public distribution system. Levy sale price is always less than open market price. Free sale sugar quota may be sold by factory in open market by inviting tenders. It is observed in the sugar factories that, the government controls the sale of sugar which slows the speed of sales. Hence, all factories have to hold huge stock of its production. This lengthens the duration of operating cycle, which results in cash shortage. Production of co-operative sugar factories are governed by sugarcane availability in its area of operation, and not by demand and supply forces in the market. The production of sugar increases as per the availability of sugarcane, irrespective of demand. This results in accumulation of huge stocks of sugar.

The growth in inventories is the common feature of all factories studied. The average growth index of inventories in co-operative sugar factories ranges between 106% and 290% over base year 1991-92. The highest growth index is shown by Manjra and lowest by Jalna.

Inventory turnover ratio of co-operative sugar factories shows that inventory turnover is less than standard ratio. The lower ratios indicate the lower efficiency of inventory management. The inventory turnover ratio ranges between 0.92 and 1.36. The higher ratio is shown by Siddheshwar and Manjra and lower by Godawari Dudhana.

Lower ratio shows inefficient use of inventories in the factories. The inventory turnover ratio analysis reveals that there was inadequate inventory in all factories studied. The highest average inventory turnover ratio observed was 1.36 in Manjra and lowest 0.92 in Godawari Dudhana. It is observed that the average highest inventory turnover ratio of 1.65 was ascertained in 1991-92 and lowest 0.82 in 1994-95.

It may be noted that the sugar factories are not free to sell the stock of sugar according to their financial needs. It is clear that the sugar factories have maintained huge stock of finished goods blocking heavy amount. It is common feature of sugar factories that they have to hold huge stock of sugar continuously for a long period.

Not a single factory touched the standard ratio of 2:1, except Gajanan in the year 1991-92. This shows low speed of sales and consumption of stores and spares. Huge stocks of sugar and stores, low rate of sales of sugar and consumption of stores and spares have slowed down the inventory turnover ratio. This reveals that there are excess of inventories in co-operative sugar factories.

4. Receivables Management

The nature of receivable in co-operative sugar factories is different. Credit sales are not permitted in sugar factories. Hence receivables in co-operative sugar factories are a composition of several items like loans and advances to employees, advances to harvesting and transportation contractors, advances for repairs and maintenance work, prepaid expenses and deposits.

The receivable turnover ratio indicates a better position of receivables management in most of the sugar factories. No serious problem about recovery of receivables noticed as all receivables occur against payment in future through which they are normally recovered. There are some problems of recovery of advances to harvesting and transportation contractors as sometimes they don't work regularly, and equal to the amount of advance paid to them, e.g. Gajanan, Godawari Dudhana, Godawari Manar and Terna. The growth rate of receivables is higher in these factories.

Receivables in co-operative sugar factories are a composition of several items like loans and advances to employees, advances to harvesting, transportation contractors, advances for repairs and maintenance work, prepaid expenses deposits, etc. It should be noted that receivables do not include debtors against credit sales as credit sales are not permitted in sugar industry. The analysis of receivables reveal that, advances to harvesting and transportation contractors and advances to farmers are the major components of receivables.

To judge the performance of receivables management, account receivables turnover ratios are computed which ranges between 4% and 12% on an average. It shows better performance of receivable management. There are no receivable against credit sales in the sugar factories. Almost all receivables are in the form of loans and advances. Loans and advances are given against proper security. Thus accounts receivable turnover ratios are better in sugar factories studied. This ratio should not be the only one indicator of performance of receivable management.

The ratio of account receivable to sales shows the better picture of receivable management of sugar factories studied. On an average, this ratio ranges between 4% and 12%. It is found that there is no much difference between the ratios of 2500 TCD factories and 1250 TCD factories.

5. Cash Management

The term 'cash' in co-operative sugar factories refers to cash in hand and cash at bank (in all bank accounts including current accounts and saving accounts).

Major cash inflows in co-operative sugar factories are from sale of sugar, sale of by-product, deposits from farmers, raising working capital loans and operative profits. Major cash outflows are for payment of cane purchases, payment of harvesting and transportation expenses, purchase of stores and spares, refund of deposits, loans and advances and payment of revenue and capital expenses.

The average growth index of cash moved between 52% and 529% in the sugar factories during the study period. The lowest growth index is of Godawari Manar and highest is of Terna. It is found that the growth indices varied during the study period in all factories. There were fluctuations in the growth indices as size of cash increased or decreased every year. This has been observed in all factories, throughout the study period. The ups and downs in cash, particularly in cash in bank, show that amounts are collected from other sources and deposited in bank for time being and again withdrawn for utilisation as per the predetermined plan.

The average cash to sales ratio is appeared highest, i.e. 8 per cent in Tuljabhavani and lowest 1 per cent in Godawari Manar. High ratio indicates good liquidity position of the factory, while lower ratio indicates the poor liquid position. It is revealed that the change in size of cash is in proportion to change in the size of sales. Increase in cash is related to sales.

The industry average of cash to working capital ratio observed was 3 per cent. The average ratio for ten years, found highest, i.e. 6 per cent, in Tuljabhavani among all the factories studied, while lowest ratio of 1 per cent was observed in Godawari Manar. Higher ratio shows a good liquid position of the factory.

The liquidity ratio analysis presents a very poor picture of cash management in co-operative sugar factories studied. It is observed that the liquidity position of sugar factories was very poor during the study period.

B. CONCLUSIONS

Working Capital Management

Working capital management in co-operative sugar factories is more significant because it is a seasonal industry. Sugar factories have limited period of work called as 'Crushing Season'.

Co-operative sugar factories have no internal source of working capital except small source of refundable and non-refundable deposits and reserves. Hence they have to depend upon bank finance for working capital every year.

Trend Analysis

All sugar factories have shown growing tendancy of current assets. They carry heavy stock of sugar throughout the year. Excess sugar stock and deficit cash are the common features of co-operative sugar factories in the region.

Working capital loan is a major current liability, which has shown continuous growth in all factories. On an average, almost all sugar factories, except Siddheshwar and Manjra showed excess of current liabilities over current assets and thus negative working capital.

Working capital trend shows a poor performance of working capital management by sugar factories. Working capital trend in co-operative sugar factories is completely different from other industries.

(a) Efficiency of Working Capital

The working capital turnover analysis indicated very poor performance of working capital. The reason behind low turnover is found that the sales are regulated by government and factories are not free to sell the sugar at their own. Selling process of sugar is lengthy and working capital turnover ratio tends to be lower in sugar factories as compared to other industries.

(b) Liquidity Analysis

The ratio analysis revealed a very weak financial position of co-operative sugar factories. The recommended current ratio is 2:1. It is observed that no factory has met the recommended ratio during the study period, except Siddheshwar in 1991-92 to 1993-94 and 1997-98.

The quick ratio recommended is 1:1 but not a single factory touched this ratio. It shows very poor liquidity position of the factories. It is observed that the sugar factories under study have been failed in equalizing the liquid assets with liquid liabilities.

The current ratio and quick ratio show very weak financial position of co-operative sugar factories. The huge stock of sugar which is unnecessarily dumped in the warehouse creates problem in finance and it affects the liquidity position of the sugar factories.

Inventory

Inventory management is an important determinant of failure or success of working capital management in co-operative sugar factories. The finished goods inventory, i.e. stock of sugar is beyond control of management of co-operative sugar factories.

Free sale of sugar is not allowed to sugar factories. All factories have to sell sugar under the control of government. It is observed in the sugar factories that the government control over the sale of sugar slows the speed of sales. Hence, the sugar factories have to maintain huge stock of finished goods blocking heavy amount.

Inventory turnover ratio shows very weak position of co-operative sugar factories. The average inventory turnover ratio ranges between 0.92 and 1.36. Lower ratio shows inefficient use of inventories in the factories. The inventory turnover analysis revealed that there was inadequate inventory in all factories studied.

All important aspects like purchase of raw material, i.e. sugarcane, production of sugar and sale of sugar are regulated by government. So nothing remains in the hands of sugar factory to manage the working capital, except getting working capital finance.

Receivables

The nature of receivables in sugar factories is different from other industries, as sugar factories permit no credit sales. Sugar factories are lagging behind in formulating return-oriented, effective and strict policies regarding receivables.

It is observed that there are some problems of recovery of advances to harvesting and transportation contractors, as sometimes they do not work regularly and equal to the amount of advances paid to them. A strict control over receivables was not exercised by most of the sugar factories.

Cash

The nature of cash management in co-operative sugar factories is entirely different from other industries. Government and banks regulate cash inflows and cash outflows in sugar factories.

It is the common practice of all the sugar factories to get additional working capital loans to meet the deficit cash. Not much cash is left in the hands of management of co-operative sugar factories, as cash inflows and outflows are regulated by government to a large extent.

Cash to working capital ratio and cash to sales ratio had been very poor in all co-operative sugar factories, throughout the study period.

The liquidity position of co-operative sugar factories is very poor as the cash inflows and cash outflows are not properly managed. The main cash inflow, i.e. sale of sugar, cannot be freely used by co-operative sugar factories. The amount of sales is directly deposited in banks against working capital loan account as per the terms of loan.

C. SUGGESTIONS

The present study observed that most of the sugar factories under study are running in losses. Financial position of the sugar factories found very weak. The experience in co-operative sugar factories in Maharashtra has proved that the agricultural processing units in co-operative sector, if managed well, can provide a good scope for rural development. In spite of this success, the co-operative sugar industry in Marathwada is facing various problems and has become a centre of criticism due to several reasons. It has been a common observation that co-operative sugar factories in the Marathwada region are lagging behind in managerial efficiency. They are unable to control their cost. Hence, major co-operative sugar factories in the region are carrying huge losses.

Considering the significant role of co-operative sugar factories in the economic life of rural Marathwada region, the present study recommends the following suggestions, based on conclusions, to improve the financial position of sugar factories and efficient control over working capital:

1. Need to create internal sources of working capital finance;
2. Sale of sugar;
3. Need to control receivables;
4. Need of proper cash management;
5. Need for more liquidity;
6. Need to improve profitability;
7. Need of expert management personnel.

1. Need to Create Internal Sources of Working Capital Finance

Co-operative sugar factories have no permanent internal source of working capital finance except a small amount of refundable and non-refundable deposits and reserves. Hence they have to depend upon the bank finance for working capital every year. Internal sources, like deposits, may be created for sound financial position. This type of deposits and funds may be created through the cane bills payable to the cane growers.

2. Sale of Sugar

It is observed that the government control over the sale of sugar slows the speed of sales. Hence all factories have to hold huge stock of its production. This lengthens the duration of operating cycle which results in cash shortage. To overcome this problem, the study recommends the factory should formulate very suitable sales policy and government should help the factories in augmenting the sales volume. Government should lift the levy quota in time and release the significant free sale quota to reduce the huge stock of sugar. It will help in uplifting the factories in all respect.

3. Need to Control Receivables

The nature of receivables in co-operative sugar factories is different. Credit sales are not permitted in co-operative sugar factories. Hence receivables in co-operative sugar factories do not include debtors against credit sales.

Regarding control over advances, it is found that strict control over receivables are not exercised by most of the factories. There is much interference of directors in policy making and disbursement of advances. But they show less interest in recovery of outstanding advances. Sugar factories are lagging behind in formulating return-oriented policies, regarding receivables. So there is need to formulate return-oriented, effective and strict policy regarding receivables, so as to recover the loans and advances in time.

4. Need of Proper Cash Management

The nature of cash management in co-operative sugar factories is entirely different from other industries. Government and bank regulate cash inflows and cash outflows of sugar factories. The factories always feel short of cash and their current liabilities exceeded current assets throughout the study period. This is the picture of almost all co-operative sugar factories in the Marathwada region. As cash inflows and outflows are regulated by government adequate cash was not left in the hands of management of co-operative sugar factories.. To improve the liquidity position of co-operative sugar factories, cash inflows and outflows are to be managed properly.

The sugar factories have maintained huge stock of sugar. Therefore, government should release appropriate quota, under free sale, to improve the cash position of the sugar factories.

5. Need for More Liquidity

Liquidity is the most alarming problem in co-operative sugar factories. It is found that there is lack of liquidity in most of the sugar factories studied. The current assets are not found sufficient for the payment of current liabilities. The main reason for this is the government restrictions on sale of sugar. Secondly, all the co-operative sugar factories are seasonal and this also affects the liquidity position of the factory. The sugar factory must pay the amount of the cane price to sugarcane grower in proper time. If factory could not pay the cane price in time, they do not believe on co-operative sugar factories.

6. Need to Improve Profitability

The data collected from selected co-operative sugar factories shows that a liberal working capital policy is adopted by co-operative sugar factories. The reason behind this may be the strong support of State Government to co-operative sugar factories sanctioning adequate finance through co-operative banks. Working capital finance policy in co-operative sugar factories is liquidity-oriented and not profit-oriented. In this period of globalization, co-operative sugar factories have to improve its profitability.

7. Need of Expert Management Personnel

The very success of these co-operative sugar factories depends upon the competence and caliber of the officers who are working at management as well as technical level. The study indicates that almost all the units have registered net losses around 4 to 9 years over a period of time. It shows that there is a need to have a competent and efficient staff at managerial level. The successful working of these units can only be achieved if there is expert management personnel.

Bibliography

1. Agrawal N.P., *Analysis of Financial Statements,* National Publishing House, New Delhi, 1982.
2. Agrawal N.K., *Management of Working Capital,* Sterling Publishers Pvt. Ltd., New Dehli, 1983.
3. Agrawal N.P. and Mangal S.K., *Reading in Financial Management,* Rupa Publications, Jaipur, 1988.
4. Ansari A.A., *Co-operative Management Patterns,* Anmol Publications, New Delhi, 1990.
5. Brandit L.K., *Analysis for Financial Management,* Englewood Cliffs, Prentice Hall, 1972.
6. Batty J., *Management Accounting,* McDonald and Evans, London, 1966.
7. Baradia S.C., *Working Capital Management,* Pointer Publisher, Jaipur, 1988.
8. Beranek William, *Working Capital Management,* Wadsworth Publishing Co. Inc., Belmont Clattering, 1966.
9. Bhalla V.K., *Working Capital Management,* Anmol Publications, New Delhi, 1997.

10. Banarjee Babatosh, *Cash Management—A Practical Approach,* World Press Pvt. Ltd., Calcutta, 1982.

11. Bari R.R. (Ed.), *Selected Readings in Cash Management,* Triveni Publications, Delhi, 1981.

12. Choudhary B. Roy, *Working Capital Management,* Eastern Law House, Calcutta, 1977.

13. Choudhary S.B., *Analysis of Financial Statements,* Asian Publishing House, Bombay, 1965.

14. Chadda R.S., *Inventory Management in India,* Allied Publishers, Bombay, 1971.

15. Choyal B.R., *Financial Management of State Enterpirses,* Printwell Publishers, Jaipur, 1986.

16. Chandra Prasanna, *Financial Management,* Tata McGraw Hill Publishing Co. Ltd., New Delhi, 1997.

17. Chakraborty, Bhattacharya, Rao and Sen, *Financial Management and Control,* MacMillan India Ltd., Delhi, 1981.

18. Dobrovoisky S.P., *The Economics of Corporate Finance,* Tata McGraw Hill, New Delhi, 1976.

19. Dean S. Ammer, *Materials Management,* D.B. Tarporwala Sons and Co. Ltd., Bombay, 1977.

20. Emerson O. Henke, *Introduction to Accounting,* Petrocelli/Charter, New York, 1974.

21. Foulke Roy A., *Practical Financial Statement Analysis,* McGraw Hill, New York 1961.

22. Franks J.R. and H.H. Scholfied, *Corporate Financial Management,* Gower Press, Epping, 1974.

23. Fremgen J.M., *Accounting for Managerial Analysis,* Homewood, Irwin, 1972.

24. Gupt L.C., *Corporate Management and Accountability Towards a Joint Sector,* Macmillan, Madras, 1974.

25. Gupta P.K., *Principles and Practice of Cost Accounting,* Agra Book Store, Agra, 1974.

26. Guthman Harry G., *Analysis of Financial Statements,* Prentice Hall, New Delhi, 1964.

27. Gupta B.L., *Management of Liquidity and Profitability,* Arihant Publishing House, Jaipur, 1994.

28. Gupta S.P., *Statistical Methods,* Sultanchand and Sons, New Delhi, 1984.

29. Gopal krishnan P., *Inventory and Working Capital Management Hand Book,* Macmilan India Ltd., Delhi, 1991.

30. Gladson, Park, *Working Capital,* Macmillan Company, New York, 1963.

31. Hingorani N.L. and Ramanathan A.R., *Management Accounting,* Sultanchand and Sons, Delhi, 1973.

32. Howard L.R., *Working Capital, Its Management and Control,* MacDonald & Evans Ltd., London, 1971.

33. Inamdar N.R., *Government and Cooperative Sugar Factories,* Popular Prakashan Bombay, 1965.

34. Inamdar S.M., *Financial Management,* Everest Publishing House, Pune, 1997.

35. Juma Volter Mwapachu, *Management of Public Enterprises is Developing Countries,* Oxford Publshing Co., 1983.

36. Jain and Mathur, *Working Capital Management,* Research and Development Association, Jaipur, 1991.

37. Jain Ravi K., *Working Capital Management of State Enterprises in India,* National Publishing House, Jaipur, 1988.

38. Joshi Vijay Prakash, *Working Capital Management under Inflation,* Anmol Publication, New Delhi, 1995.

39. Jhamb L.C., *Inventory Management,* Everest Publishing, Pune, 1997.

40. John J. Hampton, *Financial Decision-Making,* Prentice Hall of India Pvt. Ltd., New Delhi, 1980.

41. K. Venkat Janardhan Rao, *Working Capital Management in Small Scale Industrial Units,* Anmol Publications Pvt. Ltd., New Delhi, 1998.

42. Kumar Chittaranjan, *Sugar Industry Management,* Deep & Deep Publications, New Delhi, 1994.

43. Kharche R.M., *Sugar Co-operative in Developing Economy,* Parimal Prakashan, Aurangabad, 1989.

44. Kulkarni P.V., Sathya Prasad B.G. *Financial Management,* Himalaya Publishing House, Mumbai, 1999.

45. Kuchhal S.C., *Financial Management,* Chaitanya Publishing House, Allahabad, 1982.

46. Khan M.Y. and Jain P.K., *Financial Management,* Tata MacGraw Hill Publishing Co. Ltd., New Delhi, 1997.

47. Kulkarni P.V., *Financial Management,* Himalya Publishing House, Mumbai, 1985.

48. Lamer Lee Jr. and Donald W. Dobler, *Purchasing and Material Management,* Tata Mac Graw Hill Publishing Co. Ltd., New Delhi, 1978.

49. Lowrence J. Gitman, *Principles of Management Finance,* Harper & Row Publishers, New York, 1976.

50. Menon K.S., *Purchasing & Inventory Control,* Wheeler Publishing, New Delhi, 1997.

51. Murthy Varanasi S., *Management Finance,* Vakils Feffer and Simons Ltd., Bombay, 1978.

52. Maheshwari S.N., *Financial Management,* Sultan Chand and Sons, New Delhi, 1997.

53. Mathur B.L., *Financial Management,* RBSA Publishing, Jaipur, 1999.

54. Manmohan and Goyal, *Management Accounting,* Sahitya Bhavan, Agra, 1990.

55. NCAER, *Structure of Working Capital,* National Council of Applied Economic Research, New Delhi, 1966.

56. Nikam G.A., *Financial and Cost Analysis of Sugar Cooperatives,* Indu Prakashan, Pune, 1992.

57. Pande I.M., *Financial Management,* Vikas Publishing House Pvt. Ltd., New Delhi, 1994.

58. Paul S. K., *Advanced Financial Management,* New Central Book Agency Pvt. Ltd., Calcutta, 1997.

59. Rao K.V., *Management of Working Capital in Public Enterprises,* Deep & Deep Publications, New Delhi, 1990.

60. Ratnam P.V., *Ratnam's Financial Advisor,* Kitab Mahal, New Delhi, 1990.

61. Rajeshwar K. Rao, *Working Capital Planning and Control in Public Enterprises in India,* Ajanta Publications (India), Delhi, 1985.

62. Rastogi R.P., *Financial Management,* Galgotia Publishing Company, New Delhi, 1999.

63. Rao Ramesh K., *Financial Management,* Macmillan Publishing Company, New Delhi, 1987.

64. Sabade B.R. (Ed.), *Industrial Development of Maharashtra,* Maharashtra Chamber of Commerce and Industries, Pune, 1987.

65. Srinivasan S., *Cash & Working Capital Management,* Vikas Publishing House Pvt. Ltd., New Delhi, 1999.

66. Sharma N.K., *Working Capital Management,* Surabhi Publications, Jaipur, 1998.

67. Sharma R.K. and Gupta Shashi K., *Financial Management,* Kalyani Publishers, Ludhiana, 1996.

68. Sharma Uma, *Management of Working Capital,* Akashdeep Publishing House, Delhi, 1990.

69. Tupe S.D., *Sugar Cooperatives and Rural Change,* Dwarka Prakashan, Pune, 1992.

70. Tarapore S.S., *India's Financial Policy,* UBS Publishers & Distributors Ltd., New Delhi, 1999.

71. Tayadé Pushpa, *Economic Study of Sugar Industry in Vidarbha Region,* Mangesh Publication, Nagpur, 2002.

Reports and Magazines

1. Annual Reports: *National Federation of Co-operative Sugar Factories Ltd.,* New Delhi, 2000-01.

2. Annual Reports: *Maharashtra Rajya Sahakar Sakhar Karkhana Sangh Ltd.,* Nariman Point, Bombay, 2000-01.

3. *Performance of Sugar Factories in Maharashtra,* Season 1999-2000 and 2000-01, VSI, Pune.

4. *"Co-operative Sugar"* Vol. 33, March 2002, National Federation of Co-operative Sugar Factories Ltd., New Delhi.

Unpublished Ph.D. Thesis

1. Chisty M.H., *Financial Workings of Sugar Industry in India,* Ph.D. Thesis, Dr. B.A.M. University, Aurangabad, 1988.

2. Deshmukh R.D., *Creative Study of Sugar Industry under Co-operative Sector in Marathwada,* Ph.D. Thesis Dr. B.A.M. University, Aurangabad.

3. Sondge G.B., *Significant Financial and Operational Dynamics of Co-operative Sugar Industry in Marathwada,* Ph.D. Thesis Dr. B.A.M. University, Aurangabad, 1995.

Index